Design by H. V. Stephenson

The ARTISTES include—

Jean Anderson	Geoffrey Dunn	Joanna Horder	John Mott
Daphne Anderson	Clive Dunn	Hattie Jacques	Barbara Mullen
Hedli Anderson	Robert Eddison	Ernest Jay	Robert Nichols
Alexander Archdale	Lyn Evans	Megs Jenkins	Ronan O'Casey
Sydney Arnold	Jonathan Field	James Justice	Peggy van Praagh
Rosalind Atkinson	Elsie French	John Justin	Bill Rowbotham.
Frank Baker	Peter Godfrey	Lilly Kann	Leonard Sachs
Frith Banbury	John Glyn Jones	Irving Kaye	Bill Shine
Charlotte Bidmead	May Hallatt	Julia Lang	Joan Sterndale Bennett
Heather Boys	Archie Harradine	Thérèse Langfield	Fred Stone
Ian Carmichael	Elton Hayes	Lisa Lee	Eleanor Summerfield
Erik Chitty	John Heawood	Charles Leno	Tony Sympson
Alec Clunes	John Hewer	Harry Locke	Peter Ustinov
Edric Connor	Geoffrey Hibbert	Diana Maddox	Violetta
Joyce Cummings	Owen Holder	Denis Martin	Josephine Wilson
Colleen Clifford	Vida Hope	Bernard Miles	Dennis Wood
Nuna Davey			

Charman:- Don Gemmell

At the pianoforte:- Betty Lawrence & Stan Edwards

Scenery designed and painted by REGINALD WOOLLEY

Stage Director: GERVASE FARJEON

Stage Manager: MARY BENNETT assisted by VERNON RUSSELL

Ballets arranged by JOHN HEAWOOD

Costumes by PLAYERS' THEATRE WARDROBE, L. & H. NATHAN, Ltd.

Nylon Stockings by KAYSER BONDOR

Stage Lighting by MAJOR EQUIPMENT Co., Ltd.

Master Carpenter: FREDERICK DRAPER

Secretary: ENID COLLETT

Box Office: EDNA HEWER

1952

LATE AND EARLY JOYS

AT

THE PLAYERS' THEATRE

RIQUET WITH THE TUFT
A Christmas Pantomime

LATE AND EARLY JOYS

AT
THE PLAYERS' THEATRE

by
PAUL SHERIDAN

Illustrated by
REGINALD WOOLLEY

with a Foreword by
DAME SYBIL THORNDIKE

LONDON ★ NEW YORK
T. V. BOARDMAN AND COMPANY LIMITED
14 COCKSPUR STREET, LONDON, SW1

FIRST PUBLISHED 1952

14.469

PRINTED AND BOUND IN ENGLAND BY
HAZELL WATSON AND VINEY LTD
AYLESBURY AND LONDON

Contents

Acknowledgements

The Players' Theatre wishes to make grateful acknowledgement to the following: Mr. Hedley of 'The Cloisters', Windsor Castle; Mr. W. J. Lawrence of The Times; *Mr. Alan Dent of the* News Chronicle; *Mr. Marriott of* The Stage; *the British Museum; the Royal Institute of British Architects; Mr. Raymond Mander; Mr. Joe Mitchenson; Miss Jean Anderson; Miss Audrey Weir; Miss Pamela Cridge; Mr. Reginald Woolley; Mr. Gervase Farjeon; Mr. Feliks Topolski; Mr. Peter Taylor; Mr. R. Aubrey; Mr. W. Wheeler; Mr. Angus McBean; Mr. Barry Hicks; Mr. Bert Hardy and the Hulton Press.*

Foreword

HOW refreshing to have a book about the Players' Theatre and the *Joys* – our theatre literature is more often concerned with the serious drama and the ideals, successful and otherwise, of pioneer efforts. Well, the *Joys* were a pioneer effort of quite another order. When Peter Ridgeway broached the idea of the Players' Theatre to me many years ago, I thought it was more than a bit daring – it was a very new thing then, you see, this Club-Theatre idea, none of us could foresee how it would turn out. Peter Ridgeway had a very lively imagination and he did foresee that it was something people were wanting – an intelligent light entertainment of a very varied character, eatables (very nice and tasty in those days) and drinkables while enjoying the show – a lovely sort of party feeling! What varied entertainment it was too – and much undiscovered talent came along, and original ways of setting out drama.

Peter's tragic illness and death only made his friend Leonard Sachs more and more eager to keep this little theatre alive, as a sort of tribute to him – and very successfully was it run. There was artistic merit in the arrangements and performances of the programme – all praise to Leonard, who had no easy task.

But it is the later development since the taking over of the theatre in Villiers Street that has become a real part of the greater theatre of London. It is always my belief that a theatre with a policy and character has better chance of success than a theatre where the public do not know the kind of fare to be provided, and the creation of the *Joys* and its critical, sharpened viewing of the Victorian age has given a distinctive character to the Players' Theatre – a group of clever players has endeared itself to a public keenly critical, and many of the older members remember the days which the *Joys* ridicule so amusingly – and the younger ones enjoy the feeling that they are more sensible now! It is another of my beliefs that for real caricature and ridicule there must be affection for the thing or person ridiculed. Here one may say the *Joys* excel, for one comes away from their show after seeing the absurdities of certain humans – and their ridiculousnesses – feeling quite a warm affection for them and with a keener and more appreciative eye on our present-day foibles! We men and women do not alter much – we have our prejudices, stupidities and oddities in every age – now as much as in the past generations; we owe thanks to the *Joys* and those who run the theatre for making us feel a little warmer and more human to each other after taking part in one of their 'evenings'.

May the *Joys* go on and prosper – make us laugh and cry and appreciate life together – for that is the real function of the Theatre with a capital T.

SYBIL THORNDIKE

9

Victorian Supper Room

"In London I never knew what to be at,
Enraptured with this and enchanted with that;
I'm wild with the sweets of variety's plan,
And life seems a blessing too happy for man!"

HAD Captain Morris, "Laureate of the Beefsteak Club", who wrote this verse, read in the *Era Almanack* for December 12th, 1874, of the death of one John Greenmore (otherwise known as "Paddy" Green), he would, as a good club-man, have been sorely grieved. Green's death was the death also of the renowned place of midnight entertainment known as Evans's Song and Supper Rooms – forerunner of the present Players' Theatre (London's only Victorian Music-hall), under the arches by Charing Cross Station.

The exact date of the closing of Evans's is a little obscure. Burnand, in his play *The Colonel*, has one of his characters say that Evans's is closed now. The play was produced in 1881: there is evidence that the Supper Rooms were open in 1879; we must assume that they were closed (the licence having been taken away) in 1880. Six years after "Paddy" Green died, it is true, but these particular Supper Rooms had already seen their hey-day during his reign. When Green retired from the business, Evans's very quickly deteriorated. It was the end of an era in the fullest and widest sense of the term. In its narrower meaning, as applied to only one small part of the Victorian age, it was the end of a period rich in entertainment, good conversation and the fine art of enjoyment; not to be revived for another half-century.

It was from the late 1820's that the Song and Supper Rooms were really prominent in London life, and existed in all parts of the town, chiefly, of course, in the West End, anywhere between St. James's and Temple Bar. Their principal feature was the vocal and instrumental music offered to the diners and drinkers who frequented the Rooms in great crowds. At all times of the late evening and night, up to two and three in the morning, hot suppers, admirably cooked and served, could be obtained, with foaming tankards of ale or steaming glasses of grog or brandy-and-water. Meanwhile they listened as they ate and drank, and smoked the good cigars, to the strains of the comic or sentimental songs sung by the vocalists attached to the particular house. The host it was who usually took the chair at the "proceedings", and whose manner and voice contributed solidly to the harmony of the long nights.

When all this began, the entertainers were usually amateurs, chosen from the audience, but some of them had their services so frequently and vociferously demanded by the audiences that they were retained. Gradually the entertainments became professional, and were soon exclusively so.

ONE O'CLOCK A.M.:   EVANS'S SUPPER ROOMS
From "Twice Round the Clock" by G. A. Sala. 1859
FROM THE RAYMOND MANDER AND JOE MITCHENSON THEATRE COLLECTION

Evans's was among the oldest of the Supper Rooms institutions, along with the Cyder Cellars in Maiden Lane, Covent Garden, the Coal Hole in the Strand, Offley's in Henrietta Street and the Dr. Johnson in Bolt Court. Evans's led them all.

"Paddy" Green, its Chairman and Host, was a "figure", an old hypocrite and a humbug – and a showman *par excellence* in the Song and Supper Rooms he created at 43, King Street, Covent Garden, in the days of Good Queen Victoria. The house, at the end of the piazza, is believed to have been built by Inigo Jones, and listed among its earliest occupants are Killigrew, the Restoration dramatist, Sir Kenelm Digby, Lord Archer and the Earl of Stirling. The house was also very probably the meeting-place of the first Cabinet Council, under Lord John Russell.

It was a man by the name of David Low (or Lowe) who converted it into the first family hotel in the metropolis, "The Grand". The year was 1774, and the proprietorship became successively "Froome's", "Hudson's", "Richardson's", and – the name is important – "Joy's". Although W. C. Evans followed Joy in ownership of the hotel, the influence of the previous owner remained, and it was known always as "Evans's – Late Joy's". Perhaps it was that during Joy's reign the nobility had made free use of his hotel, had made of it a sort of aristocratic rendezvous, there being no West End clubs. Indeed, it has been noted, with some complacency, in several histories and diaries of the times that the large dining-room was known as "The Star", because "as many as nine members of the peerage are known to have dined there together". At all events, W. C. Evans took over a house with a considerable reputation, and was to make of it a house known throughout London – for something entirely different.

Evans had been a comedian at the Covent Garden Theatre, and certainly it seems that here lay the germ and the idea for his Song and Supper Rooms, an idea that was copied all over London; but, like most copies, lacked the fine, subtle flavour of the original. Evans flourished, and became known throughout the length and breadth of the City, "the best and the worst" flocking to Covent Garden night after night, there to drink and eat, talk and sing, or just to listen to the glee-singers and ballad-mongers on the stage at the end of the huge dining-room.

Evans retired in 1844, in favour of "Paddy" Green, also, strangely enough, an actor, this time from the Adelphi Theatre. Green, with his magnificent Chairmanship, brought the Song and Supper Rooms at King Street to full flavour. Under his management the place was entirely reconstructed and the nature of the entertainment greatly improved. A new hall over seventy feet long, and which with the old room attached made a total room length of a hundred and twenty feet, was erected to hold the vastly increased number of customers frequenting the house. Ladies were never admitted during his proprietorship; the appeal was entirely to the male element, who rejoiced in the "public privacy" of what was virtually a club. "It is a lofty, handsome, comfortable room, whose acoustic properties are far superior to those enjoyed by some establishments with loftier philharmonic pretensions. . . . As for the huge area stretching from the proscenium to a row of columns which separate it from the antechamber café, it is occupied by parallel lines of tables, which, if they do not groan beneath the weight of good eatables and drinkables piled upon them, might certainly be excused for groaning – to say nothing of shrieking, yelling and uttering other lamentable noises, evoked by the unmerciful thumping and hammering they undergo at the conclusion of every fresh exercitation of harmony" (*Twice Round the Clock*, by G. A. Sala). By midnight the place was packed to the doors, and at the tables, over chops and stout, could be seen the heavy swells, moustached, with white kid gloves, officers, the scions of noble houses, country gentlemen, merchants, lawyers, medical students and the literary men of the day, deep in talk in that part of the huge room reserved for "Conversational Parties", or sharing the applause and stamping at the "turns" as they came and went, till the tumult became a perfect storm of sound. In this room, on one night alone, there were 1,200 people, and it is recorded that they consumed 478 chops, 21 dozen kidneys, over 300 Welsh rarebits and 1,900 glasses of stout! Pandemonium was easy to let loose here, yet the Chairman, dashing his hammer to the table for silence, rarely went unheard and was never disobeyed. Among these dense crowds moved "Paddy" Green, fat, benevolent, rubicund, his eyes watchful for the important ones, chatting and joking, with a special word in their ears of this private joke or that, strutting between the tables, and achieving a popularity that neither Evans nor Joy before him had dreamed of.

In his office as Chairman of the night's entertainment, Green would sit with his back to the small stage, welcoming old friends and newcomers, the snuff-box always ready for "the gentry", exhorting with gavel and voice for the audience to call their orders. Let one of those who went there speak for himself: ". . . but the thing that did most take me was to see and hear our Ross sing the song of Sam Hall, the chimney-sweep, going to be hanged; for he had begrimed his muzzle to look unshaven, and in dusty black clothes, with a battered old hat on his crown, and a short pipe in his mouth, did sit upon the platform, leaning over the back of a chair; so making believe that he was on his way to Tyburn. And then he did sing to a dismal psalm tune, how that his name was Sam Hall, and that he had been a great thief, and was now about to pay for all with his life; and thereupon he swore an oath which did make me somewhat shiver . . . how his master had badly taught him, and how he must hang for it; how he should ride up Holborn Hill in a cart, and the Sheriffs would come and preach to him, and after them would come the hangman: and at the end of each verse he did repeat his oath, and ended by cursing them all round. . . . After Sam Hall to pay for my supper, which cost me 2/2d., besides 4d. to the waiter; and then home in a cab, it being late and I fearing to anger my wife, which cost me 2/– more; but I grudged not the money, having been much diverted" (*Mr. Pips hys Diary*). Prominent among the artists who appeared at the Supper Rooms in these days were S. A. Jones, a very fine bass singer, who was also well known at Drury Lane; John Binge, a tenor from the Adelaide Galleries and Vauxhall; J. W. "Jack" Sharp, a comedian who also used to appear at the old Mogul concert-room and at The Grapes in Compton Street, Soho. Sharp became the rage of the town, though never in the same class as Ross with his "Sam Hall". Charles Sloman, a self-styled "English Improvisatore", was another artist of fine repute. He had a wonderful knack of tagging rhymes on to any subject selected by one of the audience. Sloman was the author of "The Maid of Judah", a composition of which he was a good deal more proud than were his audiences, who grew tired of Sloman's

DON GEMMELL

15

[*Photographers Amalgamated*
SYDNEY ARNOLD

[*Feldman*
DAPHNE ANDERSON and JOHN HEWER

[*Feldman*
NUNA DAVEY

[*Gregory*
BILL OWEN

[*Gordon Anthony*

ELEANOR SUMMERFIELD

ELTON HAYES

[*Anthony Stuart*

[*Andrey Andersson*

JOAN STERNDALE BENNETT and CHARLOTTE BIDMEAD with the
COMPANY

STAN EDWARDS

AT THE
PIANOFORTE

BETTY LAWRENCE

raucous and strident singing of it. On the last occasion he is known to have sung it, he had reached the line, "No more shall the children of Judah sing", when one of his tortured listeners called out: "If they can't sing better than that, it's a good job!"

One of the long-living "familiars" at Evans's, Herr van Joel, a queer old German, sang yodelling songs and used to sell cigars among the audience, along with tickets for his final benefit night, a "night" that never came off. All the same, Joel was a real favourite there. Skinner, too, perhaps not a favourite, but certainly a man long to be remembered, was known as the "Calculating Waiter". In those days at Evans's one's bill was paid as one left the house, with Skinner standing guard at the doors, his little pad and pencil ready to tot up the meal. He was a clever psychologist. With a glance he could weigh up the nervous client, who would pay anything rather than protest, and fastening him "with a glittering eye" as he stood at the head of the out-going queue, would tot up the bill something after this fashion:

> "What have you had, sir?" – "Chop."
> "One chop, 2/6." – "Potatoes."
> "Potatoes, 3/9. Any bread?" – "No bread."
> "No bread, 4/2." – "One tankard of stout."
> "One tankard of stout, 5/10. Cheese?" – "No cheese."
> "No cheese, 6/4. Sixpence for the waiter, sir?
> "Thank you, 7/4 – 8/-. Thank you, sir! Next please."

It is not at all surprising to read that one, less nervous than another, hit Skinner over the head with a syphon of soda. Another, less violent and with a nice sense of humour, said, as the bill rose to 8/5, "One hole in the head!" – "Thank you, sir", said Skinner. "One hole in the head, 10/-. Next please!" (*Late Joys*, by Archie Harradine).

However, it was not Sala or Percival Leigh with his *Mr. Pips hys Diary*, who were to put the final stamp of authority on to Evans's, but W. M. Thackeray, that grand old penny-a-liner, journalist, avid letter-writer, poet and finally novelist, with his unforgettable portrait of "The Colonel's" visit to Evans's (retitled "The Cave of Harmony"), in his book *The Newcomes*. The Colonel takes his son, Clive, to "The Cave" to hear the good old glee-singing, under the chairmanship of the celebrated Hoskins. They join in all the choruses, the son less vociferously than his sentimental father, who laughs and grows solemn by turn at "The Derby Ram" and "The Old English Gentleman". The Improvisatore (the portrait is Sloman of course) takes them all off with his rhymes "pat to the occasion", even to the Colonel himself, and his young son:

> "*A military gent I see – and while his face I scan,*
> *I think you'll all agree with me – he came from Hindostan;*
> *And by his side sits laughing free, a youth with curly head,*
> *I think you'll all agree with me that he was best in bed!*"

The audience roars its good-natured pleasure, and the Colonel sings "Wapping Old Stairs" to the delight of all. A drunkard reels into the room, dressed in military attire. It is Captain

Costigan in his usual condition at this hour of the night. He warbles the refrain of the Colonel's song, and salutes its pathetic conclusion with a subdued hiccup.

"Bedad, it's a beautiful song," he says, "and many a time I heard poor Harry Incledon sing it." Having procured a glass of whisky-and-water from the passing waiter, and settling his florid face into a leering grin, he gives what he calls one of his "prime" songs, his legs stretched out from the chair he sits in. The unlucky wretch selected one of the most outrageous performances of his repertoire, fired off a tipsy howl by way of overture and away he went. At the end of the second verse the Colonel started up, clapping on his hat, seizing his stick, looking as ferocious as though he had been going to do battle with a Pindaree.

"Silence," he roared out.

"Hear, hear!" cried certain wags at a farther table.

"Go on, Costigan!" said the others.

"Go on!" cries the Colonel in his high voice, trembling with anger. "Does any gentleman say 'Go on'? Does any man who has wife and sisters, or children at home say 'Go on' to such disgusting ribaldry as this? Do you dare, Sir, to call yourself a gentleman, and to say that you hold the King's commission, and sit down amongst Christians and men of honour, and defile the ears of young boys with this wicked balderdash?"

"Why do you bring young boys here, old boy?" cries a voice from the malcontents.

"Why? Because I thought I was coming to a society of gentlemen," cried out the indignant Colonel. "Because I never could have believed that Englishmen could meet together and allow a man, and an old man, so to disgrace himself. For shame, you old wretch! Go home to your bed, you hoary old sinner! And for my part, I am sorry that my son should see, for once in his life, to what shame and degradation and dishonour, drunkenness and whisky may bring a man. Never mind the change, sir! – Curse the change!" says the Colonel, facing the amazed waiter. "Keep it till you see me in this place again; which will be never, by George, never!" And shouldering his stick and scowling round at the company of scared bacchanalians, the indignant gentleman stalked away, his boy after him, who seemed rather shamefaced; but I fear the rest of the company looked still more foolish; for that uplifted cane of the Colonel's had somehow fallen on the back of every man in the room" (*The Newcomes*, by W. M. Thackeray).

They were nights of noise, the noise of good conversation, of joviality and witty, trenchant repartee, when talk was a cultivated amusement. It was impossible not to sit long over your chops, or marrow bones, or hot potatoes served in a napkin, and talk and listen and join in the sing-song, right into the very small hours of morning, before leaving to pick your way through the carts stacked with vegetables to call for your cab. With the songs of the night ringing in your ears – "At Trinity Church I Met My Doom", "The Baby's Name is Kitchener Carrington", "We don't want to Fight, but, by Jingo, if we do" – the clopping of the horses' hooves over the roads to home was a fine, jigging accompaniment. Victor Listen singing the song that brought Edward VII to Evans's (when he was Prince of Wales), a song written by Henry

EVANS'S SUPPER ROOMS

From "Fun" 1865

FROM THE RAYMOND MANDER AND JOE MITCHENSON THEATRE COLLECTION

Leigh of *Punch*, was probably one of the less famous, but had with its air more than a modicum of human feeling – "Shabby Genteel":

> *"Too proud to beg, too honest to steal,*
> *I know what it is to be wanting a meal;*
> *My tatters and rags I try to conceal,*
> *I'm one of the Shabby Genteel. . . ."*

In 1860, at the height of its fame, Evans's published a free souvenir, a forty-page pamphlet, "for the acceptance of gentlemen visiting this establishment". It contains the lyrics of over a hundred of the songs, glees, madrigals and choruses sung there every night, with the names of the vocalists and musicians engaged and a detailed history of Covent Garden. "Gentlemen are respectfully requested to encourage the Vocalists by attention: the CAFÉ part of the Room being intended for Conversational Parties," reads the admonition at the head of the cover, and at the end of a list of the principal artists we find Herr Van Joel who, "in consideration of the many years of zealous assistance, will always be retained upon this Establishment" – as indeed he was until his death. Beds are advertised here at 2/–, Servants at 1/– per day! From this souvenir the writer has culled the following *jeu d'esprit*, which, though not connected with the establishment known as Evans's, deserves to be selected from the many delights of this engaging pamphlet. The correspondence first appeared in the year 1816, and was written in an effort to ridicule a great deal of the portentously serious writing encouraged at the time between the theatrical potentates of Drury Lane and Covent Garden. The pleasantries greatly contributed to restore good humour in the Green Rooms.

"Faithful Copies of Letters between Hopkins and Wild, Prompters to the Monopolisers."

Drury Lane, November 9.

Dear Wild,

For God's sake lend me a couple of conspirators for tonight. Recollect you have borrowed one of ours for a singing druid. Entirely and devotedly yours,

Hopkins.

Covent Garden, Nov. 10.

My dear Hopkins,

I have ordered them to look you out two of the genteelest assassins, and I'll take care they shall go shaved and sober. Pray tell Farren he must play our Archbishop tomorrow; we'll cut the part, that he may dress time enough afterwards for your General in "The Camp".

Yours perpetually,

Wild.

P.S.—If you have a full moon to spare I wish you'd lend it to us for Thursday. I send you some lightning that I can venture to recommend.

Covent Garden, Nov. 11.

Dear Hopkins,

Pray how shall we manage without Smith tomorrow? I depend on your lending him us for Harry the Fifth; but now I see you have put him up for Charles Surface. Couldn't you let him come to us and play two acts of Harry, as you don't want him until your third? And then Hull shall read the rest here, with an apology for Smith's being suddenly hoarse, sprained his ankle, etc.

Cordially yours,

Wild.

P.S.—My Vestal Virgin gets so cursed big, I wish you'd lend us Mrs. Robinson for a night.

JOAN STERNDALE BENNETT

[*Feldman*

[*Photo Arts*

23

[Chris Ware

[Andrey Andersson

JOHN HEWER

[Picture Post

24

Drury Lane, November 11.

Dear Wild,

By particular desire, our Vestal Virgin is not transferable, but we have a spare Venus and duplicate Juno; so send a hackney coach for whichever suits you. Your scheme for Smith won't do – but change your play to anything, for we'll tack "The Camp" to "The School for Scandal," to secure you an overflow.

Thoroughly yours,
Hopkins.

Covent Garden, November 12.

My dear Fellow,

There's the devil to do about our Tuesday's pantomime. The blacksmith can't repair our Great Serpent till Friday, and the old camel, that we thought quite sound, has broken down at rehearsal; so pray send us your elephant by the bearer, and a small tiger with the longest tail you can pick out. I must trouble you, too, for a dozen of your best dancing shepherds for the night; for though I see you'll want them for Highwaymen in "The Beggar's Opera", they'll be quite in time for us afterwards.

Forever completely yours,
Wild.

Drury Lane, November 12.

Dear Wild,

I just write you a line while the beasts are packing up, to beg you'll not be out of spirits, as you may depend on the shepherds and any other animal you have occasion for. I have it in orders to acquaint you too that we don't use Henderson for Falstaff on Friday. You may have him for Richard, with a dozen and a half of our soldiers of Bosworth Field, only begging you'll return 'em us in time for Coxheath.

Totally yours,
Hopkins.

P.S.—Lend me a cupid. Mine has got the measles.

Covent Garden, November 12.

Dear Hopkins,

Thank you for Henderson and the soldiers; do let them bring their helmets, for ours are tinning. The bearer is our Cupid, at a shilling a night, finding his own wings.

Genuinely yours,
Wild.

Amusing as are these concocted letters today, they were the rip-roaring joke of every Green Room a hundred and thirty years ago. Also in this song-book of Evans's we might be a little surprised to read a full-page advertisement that seems soundly to belie so-called Victorian prudery. It gives the details of the syllabus of one Dr. Kahn's "Philosophy of Marriage" and "Physiology of Reproduction", as delivered by him at his Museum, "top of the Haymarket, daily at 3 o'clock". The Museum itself was open "For Gentlemen Only" from twelve until five, and from seven until ten. There are other tit-bits of information and advertisement that give delight, and sometimes a faint sense of surprise at "advanced" ideas.

One final note on Evans's will suffice to give us a clear picture of the place and its popularity. It is taken from *The Train* of June 1856. "This is now a place of almost unlimited luxury. There are crystal chandeliers and . . . we have here the long desired house of late entertainment, well built, well ventilated, well conducted, well served, and therefore well patronised. We have just come in to hear 'Blow, Gentle Gales', and to get a potato . . . here it comes too, and the smoking, floury mass is in your plate. . . . 'Dere is blenty of blaces higher up, gentle-a-men,' says the time-honoured siffleur, who sells the cigars [Herr Van Joel, of course], but we courteously decline, and remain in the part of the room which is popularly known as the 'Kaffy'. You can hear the songs there nearly as well, and may converse without disturbing the company . . . the air is heavy with the smoke of cigars and loud with singing . . . the night runs on . . . and when you leave, cold and squabby is the architecture of Inigo Jones as you leave behind you the heart-warming revelry and pick your way among the dank vegetables piled on the market carts. . . . Cabby! Brompton!"

Refill the Tankards

*J*N 1880 Evans's closed its doors, and it is not until 1927 that we hear of the beginnings of the Players' Theatre. This was at 6, New Compton Street, where a club known as "Playroom 6" was opened by Miss Dorita Curtis Hayward. Here it was that Peggy Ashcroft, first of a long line of famous theatrical names connected with the Players', made her début.

In 1929, at the same address, "Playroom 6" became the Players' Theatre, and later moved to 43, King Street, as a theatre club. Towards the end of that year the Players' Theatre School came into being, still under the direction of Miss Hayward, a school teaching "the technique of the stage as well as mere acting!" In the casts of the first two plays produced here we find two young people named Harold Scott and Peter Ridgeway. In 1930 Mr. Don Gemmell put in an appearance, as Belfrage in *The Member for Turvington*, and later still as "a soldier", "Prince Julian", Shem in *Noah's Deluge*, and finally as the undescribed "Pet" in *The Siren and the Snake*. He was not perhaps aware of it then, but Mr. Gemmell was to flourish some fifteen years later as one of the three directors of the present Players' Theatre, and its Chairman and Producer. Over these early appearances he prefers, with modesty, to draw a veil!

For a short time the Players' became the Eden Club, under another management, until Peter Ridgeway, that restless genius, took it over, invested it with a brilliant idea and transplanted from another age its finest, fullest and most rewarding entertainment, the *Joys* of the Victorian age.

Ridgeway came to King Street with enough experience of theatre clubs in Greek Street and Great Ormond Street to give him the courage to start something on an almost empty pocket. Indeed, it is reliably said that the venture started on 2/6 left after the rent was paid. Less worth-while ideas have been started on much more capital, and have not achieved the deserved success reached out for and obtained by Peter Ridgeway's. With his colleague and friend, Leonard Sachs, who worked night and day with him to get the club on to its feet, Ridgeway let the theatre (called at this time the "New" Players' Theatre Club; later the "New" was dropped) for dance recitals, puppet shows, plays and the like. Along with these lettings, the Players' put on its own productions, with names among the casts that are still very popular at the present theatre in Villiers Street. There were twenty-one productions between October 1936, when the Players' opened at King Street, to the end of October 1937. It was a heart-breaking time for Ridgeway and Sachs, who not only had to produce, stage-manage and move the furniture, but also had to find the audiences! Getting people to come and sit and listen and watch the "antics" of a new theatre club was by no means easy; yet each production was exactingly done, and the membership grew. It was a year after he had moved into King Street that Peter Ridgeway began to put into execution the idea he had long nursed, a revival of the Song and Supper Room entertainments of a century before. Here he was with his theatre in the same building as Evans's Supper Rooms, with all the weight of a hundred years of tradition behind it. He approached Harold Scott for assistance. Scott, an accomplished singer, pianist and actor, had made a special study of the Victorian period, and was well known, with Elsa Lanchester, for his Victorian numbers in Nigel Playfair's *Riverside Nights*, and for their singular "Cave of Harmony" Victorian cabaret in Seven Dials. Scott was responsible for an English song-book, which contains several numbers frequently sung at the Players'. At any rate, Scott agreed with Ridgeway's plans and arranged to produce for him the first *Late Joys* night, which opened on December 6th, 1937, with the following programme:

E V A N S ' S

S O N G   A N D   S U P P E R   R O O M S

(*late* J O Y ' S)

T h e   P r o g r a m m e

(in order of their appearance):

HAROLD SCOTT in the character of JOHN CAULFIELD Jnr.		Piano duet: *Overture to Zampa*
WILFRED HANCHANT ,, JOHN CAULFIELD		
THE BOYS OF THE SAVOY CHAPEL CHOIR:		*I'd choose to be a Daisy*
(Mlles Kara Aldridge, Gabrielle Brune, Joan Collier, Patricia Hayes, Virginia Winter, Megs Jenkins)		Catches: *'Tis, I vow and swear* *Adam catch'd Eve*
HAROLD SCOTT in the character of HARRY CLIFTON:		*Paddle your own Canoe*
GABRIELLE BRUNE ,, ANNIE ADAMS:		*The Boy I love is up in the Gallery*
CHARLOTTE LEIGH ,, ELIZA COOK:		*The Old Armchair*
MEGS JENKINS ,, MISS VINCENT:		*The City Waif*
PHILIP GODFREY ,, W. G. ROSS:		*Sam Hall*
GEORGE BAKER ,, HENRY RUSSELL:		*The Maniac*
HAROLD SCOTT ,, GEORGE LEYBOURNE:		*Up in a Balloon*
RICHARD HAYDN ,, CHARLES SLOMAN:		*Ostler Joe*
BERYL MEASOR ,, MRS. FLORENCE:		*The Grecian Bend*
PHILIP GODFREY ,, THE GREAT VANCE:		*The Galloping Snob of Rotten Row*
ERIC CHRISTMAS ,, HERR VAN JOEL:		*The Singing Waiter*
CHARLOTTE LEIGH ,, MRS. CAULFIELD:		*My Heart is like a Silent Lute* (with RICHARD HAYDN)
PHILIP GODFREY ,, SAM COWELL:		*All round my Hat*
FINALE:		*Dear Old Pals*

It "took" immediately, although both Ridgeway and Sachs hoped only for a good fortnight's run. The *Daily Telegraph* set the tone with: "Peter Ridgeway's inspiration of producing a 19th-century cabaret entertainment at the Players' Theatre has captured the public in quite a sensational way." These *Late Joys* were really late night, beginning at 11.30, so that artists and audiences who had been at other theatres could join. Even later performances were given on Tuesdays and Fridays; they began at 1.30 in the morning. Naturally, the audiences for these shows were mainly theatrical, but as the news spread around that something pretty good was going on in Covent Garden, the *Late Joys* attracted Society, and "Ladies of the very brightest rank and distinction" graced the premises. "The audience is a mixture of the younger stage, a little of Mayfair and Chelsea and Bloomsbury and the Temple, and a back-wash of the old bohemian world" (*Manchester Guardian*). Even ordinary people without any magic or romance in them attended, and passed the word on. They came in with the first editions of the morning papers and went home with the milk. Despite this success, the financial strain was great on the two partners, so much so that in August 1938 Leonard Sachs thought of packing up. Ridgeway would not, and, perhaps to strengthen his morale as much as for the sake of the club, he got Leslie Banks's daughter, Daphne, to utilise the summer holiday break of that year in designing and painting murals for the theatre! These showed Evans's Supper Rooms and the National Sporting Club. When the Players' reopened, the kindly Press responded with evidence of recognition. "During the last twelve months the affable chairman of the Players' Theatre has presented to London the kind of show which every capital ought to have, namely cheap-priced intelligent cabaret" (*The Observer*). "Leonard Sachs achieves all the intimacy of a floor cabaret while he preserves the conventions of a stage" (*New Theatre*). A member of that time, and still a regular member at Villiers Street ("my grandfather was a regular patron of Evans's"), Miss A. E. Taaffe, better known as "Fudge", because of her liking for it, the chocolate variety particularly, tells a story of those days about the late Humphrey Jennings, the film director. Whenever he was in the audience, they knew with delight that there would be a witty running commentary to add piquancy to the programme. One evening Jennings was being particularly loquacious and provocative; a fellow member asked the Chairman if Mr. Jennings did not frequently remind him of Hamlet? Scenting the laugh, Leonard Sachs counter-questioned with a request for the point of resemblance, and received the reply: "Well, for one thing, he always seems to be giving advice to the Players!" So enchanted was Jennings with this retort that he went around London repeating the story against himself with gusto.

This example of badinage, common, not rare, gives one an idea of what being a chairman (and being a member) meant in those early days. Mr. Kingsley Martin, Editor of the *New Statesman and Nation*, recalls that once the war had begun and the black-out was up, if you could persuade yourself to leave your home and stumble your way through the market, barking your shins in the denseness of night, to that cellar in King Street, you were absolutely certain of meeting someone interesting, someone you had wanted to meet, or someone who, at the end of the night, you were glad to have met. "It never failed," he says, "it might have been a hand-picked audience, selected for its intelligent wit, its robust fun, its intense interest in itself and everybody else."

As funds allowed, the amenities of the club were added to, after timber and tools had been bought to make the additions. The dressing-rooms upstairs, draughtily cold, were boarded up. The solitary tea-trolley that did service for the refreshment department, grew into a real kitchen with two bars for snacks and drinks. More staff was needed, and on this matter the Players' have never been luckier than in its helpers. At that time, there were only two paid workers. All the rest were, like the artists, voluntary. The waiters were actors, and friends either stage-managed or sold tickets, or took your coat and hat. There was variety in the staff as well as on the tiny stage. Reginald Woolley spread "mystery" on the sandwiches in the snack-bar, and painted the gas brackets, as well as decorating the "ante-saloon" with Victoriana, among them being the only indubitable female Cupid known. Later he spread his wings, and brushes, to design the pantomime sets and "Spectacular Scenas" – to quote Leonard Sachs – "for which the Players' is justly famous and whose secrets Drury Lane would give a lot to know!" (*Late Joys*, by Archie Harradine). Carrying this a little further, a girl programme-seller suddenly became Principal Boy – and when Dick Whittington's Cat was called up "for the duration", the manageress of the box-office got into the skin of the part, literally, insisting (though none would accept it) that it was clearly a case of type-casting. Which member of those days does not remember "Hebe Jean" Morton, one of the very first on the staff of the Players', energetic, chatty, of whom it was said "she dispenses wine – and other comforts – to the troops". The "other comforts" in this case being her own rather special friendliness.

Artists for the *Joys* were recruited in many ways, but of particular help was Leonard Sachs's own experience in theatre. He had acted with Alec Clunes, Patricia Hayes, Geoffrey Dunn, Archie Harradine and Bernard Miles – all of whom were roped in for appearance at the Players', and who, once they appeared, had, by popular demand, to go on doing so. His remarkable energy resulted in many interesting theatrical "finds". In this way he discovered Geoffrey Hibbert in cabaret doing his own numbers, and persuaded him to "turn period", however dubious that sounds. It worked, too, for Geoffrey still appears, fifteen years later, although a lot of his time is now taken up with film work. The other half of the partnership, Peter Ridgeway, recalled appearing with Elsie French in *Little Lord Fauntleroy* six or seven years previously. She and John Mott have since become known for their Victorian pastiche, "The Aspidistras". They joined the increasing band of artists at the Players', as did Hedli Anderson, doing the Cochran show at the Trocadero. Charlotte Bidmead and Thérèse Langfield were brought in by the hand by Peggy van Praagh. They formed a trio "whose dancing in the most arch ballet since the reign of Edward VII takes the *Joys* into a very unfamiliar field" (*Star*).

Many artists also arrived by the usual auditions. They were seldom judged on any particular item heard (because rarely were such items of use to a Victorian programme), but on the possibilities seen in them by Leonard Sachs. Sometimes a suitable number was found, often it was solely a matter of production – and so to that dreaded first night when, standing in what should have been the wings but was really a space big enough for a fat cat, the Chairman called for the "Customary Warmth of Welcome to the Newest Newcomer to the *Joys*".

The never-to-be-forgotten "Sisters Gelatine" (Betty Hardy and Betty Jardine) brought their own period numbers with them; and Alexander Archdale was a pure fluke (if he'll see what I mean!), for he brought some songs for someone else to try. In no time at all he was being introduced to enchanted audiences as the "Late Music Master at Mr. Whelpington's Academy for the Younger Sons of Gentlemen". Archie Harradine, the well-beloved at Covent Garden, and later at Albemarle and Villiers Streets, was really to become "indispensable" in his successful searchings in the Charing Cross Road and the British Museum for

Drawing by Feliks Topolsk

unexpected songs, such as "The Norfolk Estuary Polka", "Cetewayo's Polka" and, of all things, "The Hippopotamus Polka". "The Aspidistras", with their roots already planted in the Victorian soil, "bloom into the heaven of burlesque" (*Observer*), and at a later date the public were adjured and artists warned that "In my view what they do should not be attempted, and could not be bettered" (James Agate). Notices from the Press became more numerous, and the name of the *Late Joys* was spread abroad. These successful productions were the result of continued hard work, finesse, good taste, style and an infinite amount of patience – with more and more hard work. Vida Hope, "a monstrous child of fabulous proportions singing 'Only a 'ittle dirly dirl', is another real treat" (*Bystander*). That original juvenile of the *Joys*, Fred Stone, was (and indeed is) "a clever young man with an effervescent manner, recalling the early days of Seymour Hicks" (*Star*). "The Jay is still with us, demanding applause and cheering himself hoarse" (*News Chronicle*). John Glyn Jones will be remembered, if for nothing else, which is very doubtful, for his Russian Grand Duke, wearing, as he carefully explained, the "Order of Chastity – Third Class – with Bar!" After describing with morbid detail the setting of "an auld Rushink folk-sonk" which he would "sink" at us, he did so with Cossack frenzy. There was Philip Godfrey with his lecture that explained how "Poesy can conquer filth" and Alec Clunes with his creation of Mr. Bassett Laneworthy-Figg, late of sundry theatres Royal. Later came Mafeking Figg and others of his extraordinary family.

A dynasty was also founded by Robert Eddison. There was the Professor who "pursued his theme, in a voice at once expiring and pertinacious, down astonishing avenues of erudition" (*Sunday Times*). But it is by his creation of the Honourable Maud Eddison that he will long be remembered. "This is Rebuke personified. . . . She treats us all as a lady should treat a pert servant. She is astonishingly evocative of novels by White-Melville, ballads by Claribel and Balfe. It is from the latter's 'fertile keyboard', in her own phrase that has emanated the song she sings, 'a not uneventful bagatelle'. . . . She is a joy of joys, her century's calm answer to our self-complacent mockery". Bernard Miles discoursing on what Beethoven said to old Mozart, or "his old rustic leaning on a wheel. This . . . is a masterpiece with real roots and radical juice in it, with the sound and smell of England in it" (*Bystander*).

Drawing by Feliks Topolski

A really startling *tour de force* was young Peter Ustinov's "lumpish, drooling, 77 years old Archbishop of Limpopoland", with "the authentic tones, the English of Oxford overlaying the faint original cockney; the slight clerical turns of phrase, never over-exaggerated; the interpolations, at every critical moment in the story, of most convincing native dialect" (*Sketch*). When, one rumbling evening in those war nights at the Players', a bomb fell, the building shuddered. The archbishop paused, mumbling sardonically, "M'mm . . . the Wright

HATTIE JACQUES

[*Keystone*

[*Photo Arts*

33

[Picture Post

The Jealous Lover

PHILIP GODFREY and SARA GREGORY

[Andrey Andersson

JOAN STERNDALE BENNETT

[Picture Post

PAT NYE and JON FARRELL

[Barry Hicks

LISA LEE

[Feldman

JOHN HEAWOOD and
LARRY DREW

34

ANNE WAKEFIELD

[*Gregory*

FRED STONE   [*Feldman*

CLIVE DUNN   [*Gregory*

The Streets of London   VIDA HOPE   [*Feldman*

35

ARCHIE HARRADINE

36

brothers have gone wrong again", and went on. Fame was his in a single night when he created the character, Madame Liselotte Beethoven-Finck. The *Bystander* found it difficult to write temperately of him. "Though only nineteen years of age he leaves such a deep impression that, well, if it had been Edmund Kean doing a stunt at a party, I should have thought it well worthy of the man who could play Richard II so superbly. It is an immense piece of acting, too macabre and too true to be merely funny, though funny it undeniably is." I feel there is little need for excusing so many quotations from the Press on the *Joys* artists of those days. Some have followed on and are with the Players' still (though often in the West End and on films). Many have climbed to greater heights than were forecast fifteen years ago.

During 1938 the Players' put on two variety shows and five plays. From the plays there was one among them that was sadly memorable – a revival of *Charles and Mary*, in which Peter Ridgeway made his last appearance at the theatre. For more than a year he had been ill, struggling to sing his songs, hardly able to recall the words of "Covent Garden in the Morning" and "Oh, the Fairies", and helped by the audience night after night, until they became the theme songs of the *Joys*. In the autumn of that year he had a serious operation, struggled to recover, failed and died on November 24th, just two weeks before the first anniversary of the *Joys*. Of him the late James Agate has written:

"I am made melancholy by the death of Peter Ridgeway at the age of forty-four. He was the kind of actor who illustrates the strength of weakness. So, too, did *Charles and Mary*, the play about the Lambs in which he made his reputation. It was a minor miracle that the play ever came to be written, and when written, produced. But the thing happened. For once in a way the key fitted the lock, and this odd, shy little actor, who was reduced to playing stammerers because of ill-health and defective memory, came to personify that other little stammerer. The impersonation of Charles was a miracle of life-likeness, tenderness, and sensibility. Now Ridgeway ought never, in this prosaic world, to have been an actor at all. First newsboy, then coffee-shop attendant, he asked and didn't take Matheson Lang's advice, joined an inferior touring company, failed, thought of becoming a monk, joined up in the war, helped at Toc H, studied for the priesthood, learned his job as an actor in Sybil Thorndike's company, started the Players' Theatre in Covent Garden, made and kept it gay, and in the heart of Lamb's own London *was* Charles Lamb. His unremarked career was a tiny edifice of which any stone might at any moment have given way. Yet poetic justice arranged that it had its tiny crown and was as complete as it could ever have been." (*Ego*, 4.)

By August 1939 the Players' was established financially, artistically and socially. There were even approaches from commercial circles for control of the theatre, which were firmly refused. It had become fashionable to bring distinguished visitors there. De Valera came, as did Alfred Lunt and Lynn Fontanne and Marlene Dietrich, as well as the entire cast of *Golden Boy*. The future, indeed, was so bright that the permanent staff was given a month's holiday with pay, reducing the bank balance to nothing. The Players' was financially disestablished once more!

A month later war was declared and all public entertainments were closed down. As the theatre had a glass roof, being on the top floor of the building, it was obvious that this was no place to be in if air-raids started, so the *Joys* moved into the Arts Theatre in Great Newport Street, dozens of sturdily loyal members helping in the move. It was difficult to find the essential sense of intimacy across footlights and an orchestra pit. When the nights proved quieter than had been feared, they returned to the fold.

Gabrielle Brune, whose song "The Boy I Love is Up in the Gallery" (the popular chorus of this is the first one played in the overture each evening), was taken to the U.S.A. by Marc Connelly, who heard her at the *Joys* and whisked her off within forty-eight hours for a new show. Richard Haydn ("The Only Living Fish Mimic") went to Hollywood to play opposite Gary Cooper in *Ball of Fire*. Megs Jenkins, seen by Bronson Albery at King Street, and engaged at once for *Story of an African Farm*, and later *The Light of Heart*; Patricia Hayes left the *Joys* to play the little servant girl in J. B. Priestley's play and film, *When We Are Married*.

One after the other their opportunities came, until a member bitingly suggested that the theatre should open as a casting agency for all theatres west of Covent Garden and all points to New York and Hollywood. "There seems these days always to be a dash of Ridgeway's *Late Joys* in West End Entertainment" (*Evening Standard*). When Wyndhams reopened, one of the first theatres to do so after the outbreak of war, six members of the cast went direct from the Players'! Peter Ustinov went into Mr. Herbert Farjeon revues, along with Joan Sterndale Bennett, Vida Hope, Joanna Horder and Bernard Miles.

The Players' first pantomime *Whittington Junior and His Cat* was produced at Christmas 1939 (it was repeated two years later), and Fleet Street took it to its surprisingly tender bosom, warmed with affection for all its delights.

PLAYERS THEATRE   COVENT GARDEN

! Extraordinary Attraction for the Christmas Season !

With a view of affording the Patrons of This Theatre every possible combination of novelty

Ridgeway's LATE JOYS

At Nine Every Evening * Except Sunday

will be followed by

WHITTINGTON JUNIOR AND HIS CAT

A MAGNIFICENT COMIC CHRISTMAS PANTOMIME

ADAPTED BY ARCHIE HARRADINE

from " WHITTINGTON AND HIS CAT " by H. J. BYRON (1862)

and " WHITTINGTON JUNIOR AND HIS SENSATION CAT " by R. REECE (1870)

Commencing Monday 18th December. ** Finishing Monday 1st January

for 2 weeks & 1 day only!

ALDERMAN FITZWARREN	Mr. P. Ustinov
P. C. BULLSEYE 1862 X	Mr. A. Harradine
BINNACLE	Mr. L. Evans
KING KOLLYWOBBOL THE 1000TH	Mr. A. Burne
DICK WHITTINGTON	Mrs. N. Davey
THE CAT	Mr. J. Moody
MRS FITZWARREN	Miss R. Atkinson
ALICE	Miss B. Mullen
SUSAN SOPPINPAN	Miss J. S. Bennett
PRINCESS POPSIWOPSI	Madlle Sterndalova

and the *whole* CORPS DE BALLET with an *incredible number* of AUXILIARIES including
APPRENTICES, SAILORS, ROSY POSIES, &c., &c ●

The whole to be followed by A GRAND

HARLEQUINADE

especially devised by *Mr.* M. WILLSON DISHER

THE NEW AND EXTENSIVE SCENERY has been expressly designed and painted by
MESS. A. FARMER and R. WOOLLEY

MR. S. YOUNG WILL PRESIDE AT THE GRAND PIANOFORTE
The Entire Evening under the Direction of **Mr. L. SACHS**

Members Free; Guests 2/6. On NEW YEAR'S NIGHT the charge to Guests will be 5/-
BOOKING IN ADVANCE IS ESSENTIAL——Temple Bar 1149 & 1780

---

* On Fridays performances are at 8.30 and 11.30, the latter in aid of
EMPIRE SOCIETIES' WAR HOSPITALITY COMMITTEE.

** *On which night all FREE privileges, excepting those of the Public Press, must be suspended.*

GOD SAVE THE QUEEN

Throwaway of the first Players' Pantomime, 1939

The raids on London began, and the Players' landlords behaved not at all as landlords are supposed to behave, and allowed the theatre the use of the basement shelter. A dais and piano were put in, and the show went on. Very soon, however, the raids became more regular, and Messrs. Munro's employees were in need of the shelter. Was this the end? No. Francis Iles (Anthony Berkeley) threw his large St. John's Wood house open: the faithful few followed the Players' there, even from as far as Chelsea in the height of the raids! Within a week this pillar-to-post "work out", ruinous to costumes, temper and morale, came to an end, with the lease of the basement of number 13, Albemarle Street, Piccadilly, offered to them – due mainly to the untiring determination of the Secretary, Pat Hill. It was a safe billet for the duration, unless five floors of reinforced concrete gave way.

The premises had formerly been the El Morocco night-club. The *Joys*, now not so "Late" as formerly – performances began at 7.30 each night, with two extra at 5.30 Tuesdays and Fridays – opened here with a different, but hardly less vociferous, kind of bang than the many that resounded through London. Nothing at all could put a stop to that particular gaiety; nothing could blast the choruses or stem the quick-witted sallies. Sachs's effervescent vitality and flow of repartee gave him a well-deserved reputation with his uncanny knack of handling all types of audiences (and they were all types!), and making them forget the blitz with a vitality and a friendliness that gave as much to the entertainment as did the artistry of the company gathered there night after bomb-wrecked night.

Soon the Players' began to pay its artists salaries that compared well with those of other, more prosperous and commercial theatres. The war was on and the theatres shut down – but not the Players'; that went on merrily through blitz, fires and many natural forms of intimidation. It must be admitted, all the same, that the theatre personnel became infected with its own crisis inside the immense crisis of war. Leonard Sachs received his calling-up papers for overseas draft. Immediately he gave complete authority for the control of the theatre into the hands of Jean Anderson, who as war-time Director would have to take all decisions as to the running of the theatre, its possible closing against all their wishes or its transfer to "other haunts".

With a naïveté that the emergency of the times will surely excuse, they both entirely overlooked the fact that such a transfer of authority would bear little weight with bank managers, those invulnerable and omnipotent gods. None the less, the documents were prepared. They were signed and witnessed, with that last careless fling at fate and the dogs of war, in the taxi that took Leonard Sachs from his barracks in Kensington to Victoria Station and beyond, with one of his suitcases for a "desk" and an almighty fear for the future in both their hearts.

Very quickly, under Jean Anderson's management, the Albemarle Street H.Q. of the Players' became the haven of many Service men on leave. Their letters to her bear testimony to its heartwarming (and one dares say, in some instances, heartbreaking) interludes. The Services Welfare Committees brought parties of wounded soldiers time and time again to the little cellar not far from Piccadilly, and post-cards, letters and photographs show how much these free entertainments meant to them. Indeed, in those days the Players' had a very special meaning as a rendezvous in the lives of many on active service, and they came there through black-out, bombs, rain and fog, away from the time of Hitler, back to the time of Kruger. The atmosphere was cheerful, the programmes consistently entertaining. It was Herbert Farjeon who wrote: "Leonard Sachs has now and for the duration vacated the chairmanship, but audiences are as packed as ever, and not only does Don Gemmell step valiantly into the official breach, but the artists remain to do their stuff . . . not once have I heard it complained that the performers are not up to scratch; it is, perhaps, the charm and variety of their personalities more than anything else that saves 'the Victorian joke' from becoming the bore that might so reasonably be expected, and is, in fact, so rarely experienced" (*Tatler and Bystander*).

Jean Anderson and Don Gemmell, who was in charge of productions and had taken over the chair, gave Daphne Anderson and Hattie Jacques their first contracts in the *Joys*. Hattie was then only nineteen; but she had exactly the right personality, the gaiety and the warmth – though her voice gave rise to some doubts. It was that "little girl" voice the present Players' audiences have learned to wriggle over in joy, which at that time was a natural tone and strength, and barely reached to the back of that tiny auditorium. Those members who in these times are in the habit of seeing the *Joys* from the bar on the shelf of the Villiers Street theatre may not be inclined to believe this, when every syllable of her robust ballads reverberates on the eardrums as she sets the house in a roar. Archie Harradine, Joan Gates (that happy soul, of whom Marie Lloyd would strongly have approved), Vida Hope, Joan Sterndale Bennett were among the regulars who led the audiences stamping and shouting the choruses, against that other chorus from the guns outside and far away.

Towards the end of a gentle letter to Jean Anderson, whose kindliness seemed wide and deep enough to embrace "all sorts and conditions of men", a young sub-lieutenant wrote at this time: "The Players' has been and always will be my home from home, and I can only say, with Sebastian: 'I can no other answer make but thanks, thanks; and ever thanks' . . ."

On August 24th, 1942, the Maximilian Society gave its Birthday Party to Sir Max Beerbohm at the Players' Theatre. Jean Anderson arranged the programme, and Desmond (now the late Sir Desmond) MacCarthy was in the Chair. (Not the *Joys* chair of course, that was under the benevolent gavel of "their very own" Don Gemmell.) "The Players' company splashed in a vividly coloured background of Victorian songs and recitations" (*Manchester Guardian*).

Alan ("Jock") Dent, Secretary of the Society and Dramatic Critic to the *News Chronicle*, wrote a charming letter to Jean Anderson following this event, in which he said: "Are you aware that, in the cause of our Party, Robert Lynd and I each – as it were by accident – consumed a *septuple* whisky (seven being the Maximilian number). When all was over I joined him in yet another one. 'You must make it one over the seven, Jock!' said he."

And the regular show went on, and that right royally. Every night, from the moment the candles were lit on the Chairman's table, and Don Gemmell strode across the stage in surtout and cravat with his roaring "GOOD-evening-ladies-and-Gentlemen". Sitting there on "Red Velvet 5", balancing your soup and your mushroom pie on your knees, with your mug of beer on the ledge above you, the atmosphere getting hazier and hazier with smoke, the rattle and hum of conversation dying down suddenly, you joined in the anthem of the Players' – "Covent Garden in the Morning", that joyous memorial to the first artist of them all, Philip Ridgeway. That tiny building, everyone's home from home, jammed, as it was, "to

The Aspidistras: – John Mott & Cornelius Fisher

Drawing by Feliks Topolski

the ceiling", every bit of floor space taken, could not contain anything like the crowds that besieged its doors each night. Generals, members of the peerage and "the common herd" pleaded in vain as they were turned away. Joan Sterndale Bennett singing "Johnnie Morgan plays the Organ" set the tone, and put you in proper humour for one for whom only one word was (and is today) his identity – "Indispensable". Archie Harradine, with "The Cheerful 'Arn" or "Captain Gingah". Megs Jenkins, Heather Boys, Geoffrey Hibbert, Robert Eddison – they were all there for your delight. Of Eddison a story is told of a member who had heard that "the Honourable Maud" had been called up. Apparently the eyes of the member, and indeed all his senses, had been utterly deceived by the portrayal on the stage, for he seriously and sincerely inquired of "Maud" if she was "for the Wrens"!

Two more of the most popular artists ever to appear at the *Joys* in those, and these, days are Elsie French and John Mott, "known in other and lesser haunts as 'The Aspidistras'." The solemnity of their "merry" song, "Welcome, Thrice Welcome", is Victorian parlour to the life. These constant harbingers of joy in the *Joys* radiate what *Punch* has called "the very genius of the genteel drawing-room".

Betty Lawrence and Frank Baker were "at the pianoforte", and when Don Gemmell had brought your attention and your applause, and had told you his story, the world at war made only the faintest intrusion. In those days you might "stay, and eat, and drink, and dance (and very welcome too), but after that, should there be any outside disturbances, natural or unnatural, you may stay for just as long as we can make you happy, warm and comfortable".

They were joyous nights, whatever went on outside and beyond that tiny cellar.

Players' pantomimes are now an institution, and *St. George and The Dragon* in 1942, followed by *Cinderella* the next year, were given glowing reviews by every section of the Press. "We laugh with as little restraint as any Victorian Music-hall audience" (*New Statesman and Nation*).

"Bristling with shattering puns and outrageously rhyming couplets, the 'grandiose scenery' and 'mellifluous music' are entirely in keeping with the atmosphere" (*The Queen*). Both pantomimes were adapted by Archie Harradine and were produced by Don Gemmell. A specially well-deserved tribute was paid to Reginald Woolley, for his "sets, in the appropriate splendours of old Tivoli baroque" (*The Times*). Christmas 1944 brought *The Sleeping Beauty in the Wood*, adapted and produced by the same two people, with Daphne Anderson ("prettiest of them all – and then prettier") as Fairy Rosebud, Joan Sterndale Bennett as Fairy Baneful, Don Gemmell as Thomas (surnamed Noddy), Jean Anderson as his Consort, Queen Serena, and a whole host of *Joys* talent, "amusingly mounted by this familiar and popular team, with a charming, smiling grace, and without buffoonery (*The Observer*).

In April 1945 the programme was broadcast in "Variety Bandbox" from the Queensbury All Services Club. Leonard Sachs, now returned from the wars, "was largely successful in making the broadcast seem like a complete recapturing of the period" (*Empire News*). In fact, whatever they did, and wherever they went, they rolled back the curtain a hundred years and set the scene, with all its colour and sound, of those great Victorian nights. Many shows were given before Sunday audiences at dozens of camps and in hospitals. One memorable performance was given in the chapel of a hospital – with the Chairman in the pulpit!

Yet Albemarle Street was its home. Here the famous mingled with the unknown and evening dress seemed no more fitting than khaki. The "times were out of joint", but not so those "habituées and sons of habituées", whose nightly haunt was an address the cabbies knew so well. Fame, and the word is the right one, came out of obscurity, as the Players' itself came out of that Supper Room known as "Evans's – Late Joy's", over a century before.

FRED STONE
[*Gregory*

Above left:
CLIVE DUNN
[*Gregory*

CHAIRMEN

of the

LATE JOYS

[*Feldman*

JOHN HEWER

[*Barry Hicks*

LEONARD SACHS

BILL SHINE
[*Gregory*

[*Gregory*

JOHNNY LADD

45

The Amiable Mrs. Luke

Players, Please

From This Day Forward

Calcutta in the Morning

The Cave and the Garden

AND A REVUE

Players, Please

Photos: Houston Rogers

VIDA HOPE

RONNIE HILL and THE
COMPANY

ELEANOR
SUMMERFIELD

EDMUND WILLARD

MARY LAURA
WOOD

MAY HALLATT and DON
GEMMELL

The Castle Spectre

Photos: Feldman

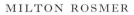

The Spectre:
PRUDENCE RENNICK

MILTON ROSMER

MARY BENNETT
Stage Manager

[*Keystone*

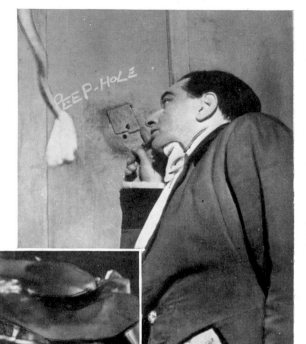

[*Keystone*

DON GEMMELL
Producer and Chairman

BACK

VIDA in
the Dressing Room

BETTY lights the candles

[*Gregory*

[*International News*

REGINALD WOOLLEY
Scene Designer

[*Feldman*

[Feldman
GERVASE FARJEON
Stage Director

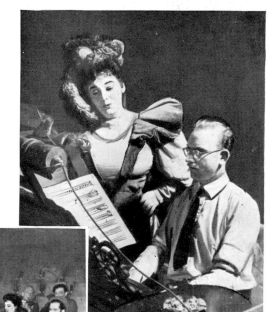

[Picture Post
HATTIE and STAN try a
new number

STAGE

[Andrey Andersson
TEA

[Photo Arts
BILL DRAPER

[Photo Arts
ANNE

[Gregory
DENNIS WOOD in the Wardrobe

49

Beauty and the Beast

HATTIE JACQUES, JOAN STERN-
DALE BENNETT, ERIK CHITTY,
DAPHNE ANDERSON

Ali Baba and the Thirty-nine Thieves

GAVIN GORDON

HATTIE
JACQUES

ERIK
CHITTY

JOHN
HEWER

JOHN HEAWOOD, JOAN STERN-
DALE BENNETT, TONY SYMPSON

HATTIE JACQUES, DAPHNE
ANDERSON, JOHN HEWER,
ERIK CHITTY

[Photos: Feldman

50

MIMES

Cinderella

[*Houston Rogers*

BILL SHINE

JOYCE
CUMMINGS

DON
GEMMELL

STEPHEN BLAKE

JOHN HEWER

DAPHNE
ANDERSON

ERIK CHITTY

CHARLES LLOYD
PACK

DAPHNE
ANDERSON

Riquet with the Tuft

HATTIE JACQUES, JOHN
HEAWOOD, JOAN STERN-
DALE BENNETT

[*Photos: Feldman*

ERIK CHITTY, JEAN ANDERSON

Harlequin
JOHN HEAWOOD

Columbine
CHARLOTTE BIDMEAD

Fairy Queen ROSE HILL

Pantaloon
BILL SHINE

Clown
JOHN HEWER

[*Photos: Feldman*

Fairy Queen HATTIE JACQUES

[*Houston Rogers*

Designed by REGINALD WOOLLEY

[*Photos: Feldman*

FRONT OF HOUSE

Eddie

Audience

Bar

Gerhard

Bruce

Supper Room

[Photos: Picture Post

54

[*Gregory*

[*Picture Post*

The Shelf

Full House

[*Picture Post*

The Toast [*Gregory*

[*Gregory*

NORDA

[*Andrey Andersson*

[*Picture Post*

GLADYS

Snack Bar [*Picture Post*

[*Weston*

HERMIONE
GINGOLD
1952

[*Mirrorpic*

QUEEN VICTORIA'S BIRTHDAY
CAKE

[*Mirrorpic*

DAME SYBIL THORNDIKE
1951

Underneath the Arches

N moving from Albemarle Street to Villiers Street, Charing Cross, the Players' Theatre had moved from one historic district to another. At the time that Evans's Supper Rooms in Covent Garden were beginning to attract the attention of writers, artists and young men-about-town – that is, the early 1800's – there was no embankment to the River Thames. Had you stood with your back to the Shot Tower and the South Bank on the other side of the river, the Villiers Street of those days would have been a very pleasing sight. The Hungerford Market, where Charing Cross Underground Station now stands, had a causeway entrance extending into the river itself. The front had a central colonnade, with a balustraded terrace, and was flanked by two handsome buildings with flat roofs. These were taverns, from where the delightful scenery of the slow-flowing Thames could be watched.

Today the almost-Venetian front of the embankment of the 1800's has entirely disappeared, and Villiers Street, viewed from the entrance to Charing Cross Underground Station, needs more than a little imagination to make its prospect please. Walking up towards the Strand, we find the Players' Theatre set back on the left-hand side of the road, and the other buildings on either side, brightly painted, its ornamental "brick" work an immediate attraction, even though the immense wall that towers above it does give it a flat, unlived-in appearance. This is the building into which the Players' moved on that rewardingly successful evening in 1946.

Formerly, way back at the end of the last century, it had been Gatti's Under-the-Arches Music-hall, opened in the 1860's by Carlo Gatti, who also ran a similar establishment in the Westminster Bridge Road, and at which such famous artists as Charles Coburn and Charles Sloman had appeared; Sloman, our "English Improvisatore", closely associated with Evans's Supper Rooms.

Gatti opened the place as a music-hall in 1867, following his proprietorship of the "Coffee and Ice Rooms" in Hungerford Market. He made a lasting name for music-hall in the building where the Players' Theatre is now housed. "Those inveterate Londoners, the Gatti's, [have] built a music-hall here . . . you pay for your glass of beer and a cigar, and then are admitted free to have as rowdy an entertainment as ever raised cain in London. My father's favourite story was of a boisterous night there when things were going from bad to worse, despite all the Chairman's bawling and thumping. When at last he did make himself heard he threatened to clear the gallery as a warning to the equally noisy but opulent people at tables on the floor; then in an ominous hush he announced the next turn, 'the elegant and tuneful Miss Spankers' who would give them 'a real good treat' with her top notes. . . . 'Oh, no, guv'nor,' rang out the immediate response, 'not that, for gawd's sake, not that, we'll be good!' " (M. Willson Disher, *Pleasures of London*). That was real music-hall in the good old days, brought to Charing Cross by an Italian who became more of a Londoner than the cockney. Carlo and his brother Giovanni managed everything themselves, standing shirt-sleeved at their desk, and were familiar figures in this London of the past. They lived on the principle of Charles Dickens's honest grocer, Mr. Barton, who made it his boast that "he was never above his business, and he hoped his business would never be above him!" The Gatti's were among the pioneers of restaurants in the city, and did a great deal towards reforming them from the disreputable places they were. Their music-hall nights were, quite evidently, lively, which might give reason to *The Times* tirade against this form of entertainment: "Their entertainments are vulgar in tone and sentiment, when they are not worse." (This is not, of course, a reference to Gatti's in particular, but to music-hall generally.) "They hover on the frontier between the tolerable and the intolerable. At best the recollection of the evening's diversion leaves a bad taste in the mouth. Apart from all their evils, they have the flagrant vice of separating class from class in its amusements. . . .

"It is much to be wished that some music-hall proprietors themselves could be persuaded to improve gradually the character of their entertainments as to render them deserving of a less exclusive patronage. The existence of a music-hall testifies that the people have ears and minds to be amused. Its frequenters take the past time it offers because they can afford nothing more elevated. Probably they would go still more eagerly to the Opera if they could pay its prices like their betters" (*The Times*, October 14th, 1883).

Music-hall had taken a firm hold not only in London but up and down the country throughout the provinces. The riotous nights at Gatti's were not only a sign of the times, much less a sign of the division of classes, but were a sign of the newest and latest form of entertainment, leading straight from the Supper Rooms, the Cyder Cellars and the Coal Hole, the vanguard of the music-hall. At Gatti's the jovial Chairman did much to restore the waning glories of his office, and there were few men more deservedly popular than this excellent good fellow . . . who won distinction for himself as a comic singer. His sturdy, thick-set figure earned for him the sobriquet of "Young John Bull". They are gone now, these evergreen sons of Bacchus, whose great good humour and vast expansiveness, like their own ebullient nature, renewed itself night after night.

Gatti's glory departed, and the Hungerford Arch became a cinema, and was finally occupied by E.N.S.A. during the '39 to '45 war. The Players' then stepped in and gave to it, not a new glory, but a revived ebullience and life, awakening echoes of those earlier days with their "Slap! Bang! Here We Are Again!" and the roaring choruses from a faithful audience. The Chairman's office has come again into its own, a position of almost unlimited power, in the very best and jovial sense.

> "*I occupy the Chair, boys,*
> *By jingo, I'm all there, boys,*
> *With my rat-tat for order, boys,*
> *I'm the idol of the Hall!*
>
> *When eight-o-clock is striking, the performance I begin*
> *With a sentimental song or two to sing the people in;*
> *And having done my turn I take possession of the Chair,*
> *And all admire my shirt-front, snowy studs and curly hair!*"

It was Frederick (Bill) Draper, Master Carpenter, who found the premises the Players' Theatre were later to occupy in Villiers Street. It was close to Charing Cross Underground Station and directly underneath the Main Line Station. Dozens of possible places had been seen all over London, but for one reason or another had been unsuitable. When Bill Draper looked out one morning from a back window in Leonard Sachs's flat in Craven Street, he saw the back, blank wall of what looked like a warehouse. In fact, the place had been a cinema, the "Forum", where "advanced" or "progressive" films were shown to the intellectuals of the late 'thirties. Enquiries were made immediately, and it was found that E.N.S.A. were in occupation. The arch had become an enormous storehouse for cinema equipment of every kind.

The war was over. Materials were in short supply and labour was difficult to get. . . . But Leonard Sachs signed the tenancy agreement. The necessity of performing a miracle fell into the astonishingly ready hands of the Albemarle Street members, and of course the staff. Night after night announcements were made in the "just off Piccadilly" haunt, and day

Watergate Walk in the Eighteenth Century

Players' Theatre

Watergate Walk Today

WOOLLEY

after day at Villiers Street, under Bill Draper's watchful eye, there arrived the strangest assortment of people who were willing to fetch and carry, to mix paint, scrape walls, heave sacks of cement about, and do the hundred and one jobs essential to making the arch habitable and usable again as a place of entertainment. Soldiers on leave came; two memorable sergeant-majors stood about having long talks about how best to "attack the situation" from what was presumably the military point of view. The work went on, feverishly and with an enthusiasm that showed how grateful members of the Players' were for their haven-on-leave during the war years. Perhaps that is why this unusual Club Theatre is so friendly a place. Not of course that there ever is any back-slapping, with new members being welcomed with ostentatious displays. Friends keep themselves to themselves; but when the place is packed, as it invariably is from Thursday onwards, it has an atmosphere, an "air", a sense of the period it represents, that gives a warmth and colour and a vivid life. Those early days at Villiers Street were days of ordered chaos, if the phrase be permitted, with Bill Draper working from morning to late night, with a gang of volunteers, to catch up with time and do the impossible – as the impossible is done under these circumstances.

The floor was raked to three-quarters of the length of the arch, and a balcony, now called the "Shelf", was added at the back. The work was started and completed by a young man, then unknown, who was working as a bricklayer in order to pay for his singing lessons. His name is William McAlpine, and today he is one of the leading tenors at Covent Garden.

It would probably be very far from the truth even to suggest that every day all the voluntary workers of the Players' at that time were happy from morning until night. Tempers were frayed on many occasions as difficulties had to be faced and overcome. Yet life had its moments of sheer fun and of curious wonderment, inside as well as outside the theatre.

On the forecourt there was a row of barrows, from which flowers, fruit and vegetables were sold. There were roast-chestnut vendors, too, who did a roaring trade with the audience when the theatre eventually opened.

At the back of the theatre, however, a less obvious "life" went on. There, in that narrow alley on to which the stage-door opened, there lived and moved the tramps of the district, who looked – at least one hoped – far more evil than they were. Their ways were strange and their habits uncertain. Now and again one of them found his way into the theatre, having "mistaken" the stage-door of the Players' for the door leading to his tramps' shelter in another arch farther along.

It was one of these characters who carried on a mysterious trade with his fellows, in the dark corner of the alley, where he partly concealed himself behind a ready-made screen of wood and sacking. All that is known of his strange activities is that behind this, day after day, he made a little fire on which was a tin – or was it a pan with the handle broken off? In the middle of the morning tramps would shuffle and sidle down to him, and round his rude screen they would hand to him handfuls of cigarette stubs which they had collected the night before from the pavements and gutters of the district. Then they would go quietly away, for he would not allow any of them to see what he did. He was, however, on one occasion seen to break open the cigarette ends and spill the tobacco into the pot, and pour on top of them some liquid or powder. This unhealthy brew he let stew for some time, meanwhile slowly stirring it, gazing into the mess as he did so. After a time he took the pot from the fire, emptied out the contents on to carefully spread-out sheets of newspaper, also collected and brought to him by his fellow wanderers. Later in the morning he sifted and sorted the dried mixture, rolling it into cigarettes, which he sold, a few at a time, to each of them as they slippered and shuffled along to his "shop". They then returned, to sit against the wall of the alley, smoking without speaking the cigarettes that seemed to give a greater satisfaction than any they might buy in any tobacconist's. For many weeks this strange ritual went on, then, as suddenly as it had all begun, it stopped, for the tramps were collected one night into vans and taken away to other, and one hopes, more salubrious quarters. Who he was, where he came from and where he finally went no one ever knew, but this alchemist left behind him a flavour of something more than mildly unpleasant, perhaps of something faintly evil, carried out as it was with such penetrating concentration, care and secrecy. A part of the hidden life of London, he leaves behind a vaguely disturbing memory, emphasising the malignant character of an alley-way that, still earlier in the century, had shrouded the corpse of a young woman found there murdered late one night.

These intrusions into the work which was going on within the theatre were soon forgotten when the Players' finally opened wide its doors for a triumphant first night. The really remarkable achievement of a band of **paid and** unpaid helpers proved itself by the audience reception on that night and the Press reception on the following morning.

"The dear Players' are back in West Central again. They have taken the old Forum cinema in Villiers Street and converted it into a new home for 'Evans's Late Joys', as near to Covent Garden again as makes no matter. It is bright and pink and noisy and suitable. Kipling, in 1889, noted of Gatti's Music Hall on this self-same sight that it had 'the smoke and roar and good fellowship of relaxed humanity'. Well, here we are again!" (*News Chronicle*). "The uproarious co-operation of the audience that filled the seats and packed the gangways . . . no fresh recommendation is required for the bucolic satire of Mr. Bernard Miles, the crinolined hedonism of Miss Nuna Davey, and the boundless versatility of Mr. Archie Harradine. These three on the opening night led the vanguard of a full muster of the leading war-time upholders of the *Joys*" (*The Times*). "Extraordinary scenes of riotous enthusiasm were witnessed 'underneath the arches' in Villiers Street, Strand, last Monday evening at the reopening of the Players' Theatre. To the strains of 'Slap! Bang! Here we are again!' the huge audience shouted itself hoarse, and this wonderful entertainment, which had successfully withstood so many transplantations, was rapturously launched in its new home" (*Morning Advertiser*).

"The best rehearsed and most nostalgic audience in town was enraptured by an opening night at which Leonard Sachs officiated as Chairman, and many artistes repeated past successes. . . . Here it is all over again" (*Daily Sketch*). "The most virile and sustained performance of the evening was given by the audience, who sang every chorus lustily and yelled themselves hoarse with excitement. . . . The Players' has become an institution in London night life, proving that variety can be intelligent, as well as entertaining" (*Stage*). And so on, and so on.

Without a doubt the Players' had a most successful launching, and that first fortnight in Villiers Street saw a complete change of programme every night. All the old "names" turned up during those first two weeks, and the formidable list included all past and present artists of the *Joys*. One has really to leave unsaid, but not, I hope, unimagined, the story of the organising zeal which lay behind the effort needed to gather them all in and ensure that they appeared. None was unwilling, on the contrary, but commitments, plays, rehearsals, auditions, jobs of all kinds combined to upset Sachs's plans. But in spite of all this he achieved what he had set out to do, and in those two memorable weeks old memories were revived and many new friends made. No one who was on the staff at that time will ever forget the Players' first fourteen days after the *Joys* opened – the crammed and as quickly emptied skips of suits, dresses, hats; the umbrellas, canes, crops, the shoes, crinoline-hoops and wigs that passed from artist to artist, made a procession, to which unidentified bodies were attached! And the artists' searchings for mislaid props, the short tempers, the packed, suffocating dressing-rooms, the eternal smell of grease-paint that seemed to cling to the very air, the stifling sense of urgency, the longing to get it over quickly, the hectic, turbulent, hardly-to-be-endured moments before the Chairman's wittily affectionate welcome brought you out there with the resounding crash of his hammer.

Downstairs, settled back in his chair in the cloakroom, is Andy, surrounded with the hats, coats and umbrellas of all who are in tonight: Andy, known to them all from Albemarle Street days, whose deservedly proud boast it is never to have lost even a handkerchief belonging to a member while he was in charge of his job, clasps fingers across his waistcoat and stares through thick-lensed glasses – into the future or the past? From the bar Eddie Green quietly removes to the back the empty crates of bottles, and, even when the house-lights are down for a particular number, does double-Dutch arithmetic that only he can understand! The last day of that fortnight, Saturday, January 26th, must have brought a great sigh of relief from everyone – except the audience, who laughed uproariously over Peter Ustinov's "Bishop of Limpopoland," who sentimentalised with Archie Harradine, and stared in a caught fascination, straining for every word spat viciously from the unrepentant, vengeful "Sam Hall" of Philip Godfrey. Graceful Charlotte Bidmead with her elegance and charm, and that great favourite of today's *Joys*, Hattie Jacques, sent them home unwillingly, and the most exacting two weeks in the history of the new Players' was over.

E.N.S.A. still occupied much of the building, and productions were difficult to put on because of this. It was not until October 1945, however, that the last projector was removed and the Players' could call their "home" their own. Now began the struggle, both to survive and to prosper, to hold fast to the old members while bringing in the new. Many of the older ones seemed to miss the intimacy of Albemarle Street, and felt that in this great arch of a theatre the *Joys* might perhaps lose its identity, and become swallowed up by something that was more than, in the merely architectural sense, bigger. What they did not realise was that the expansion of the theatre here at Villiers Street was the only possible hope the Players' had of continuing its enviable history. Too many "Little" theatres have foundered for purely economic reasons, and it is very doubtful whether the Players' could have maintained itself for long after the war if they had not made this move to larger premises. Rents had gone up, so had the cost of materials; so, too, had the salaries which had to be paid. The *Late Joys*, housed as they had been in a building with room for an audience of less than 200, would soon have had to close. The move was therefore both necessary and wise, since an increasing membership had to be catered for.

Inevitably the Players' did lose something in the move to a larger theatre, but it is also true, however, that the genuine Supper Room entertainment has been re-created, with all its punch and loud vulgarity, its bursting vitality and its utter sincerity. Who in these days can listen to and sing with Joan Sterndale Bennett, without thinking of that earlier "Vital Spark", the small and lovely Jennie Lee? Or who can hear and watch Hattie Jacques without recalling instantly the great Marie Lloyd, or watch Johnnie Heawood and not think of G. H. Elliott? Has Philip Godfrey not also caught something of A. G. Vance, that brilliant dancer and character vocalist, with his "Chickaleery Cove"?

> "*I'm a chickaleery bloke, with my one, two, three,*
> *Vitechapel was the willage I was born in;*
> *To catch me on the hop, or upon the tibby drop,*
> *You must get up werry early in the morning . . .*"

The Aspidistras—ELSIE FRENCH and JOHN MOTT

GEOFFREY DUNN
[Keystone

[Gregory
CHARLOTTE BIDMEAD
and ROBERT NICHOLS

[Feldman
VIOLETTA

[Feldman
RONAN O'CASEY and JOAN
STERNDALE BENNETT

[Gordon Anthony
GEOFFREY HIBBERT

LARRY DREW

[Gregory

DIANA MADDOX

[Anthony Stuart

DENIS MARTIN

[Gregory

IAN CARMICHAEL

[Angus McBean

JOAN STERNDALE BENNETT
JOHN HEWER

[Gregory

LISA LEE, DENNIS WOOD

[Feldman

JOHN HEAWOOD

[Andrey Andersson

[Gregory

[Feldman

How like the great George Leybourn, John Hewer is at the Players' today, with his "heavy swell", "lady-charmer" affectations, and his rip-roaring "For me, for me" and "Where did you get that hat?" Here is an artist moulded in the fine tradition of genuine music-hall.

And so one could go on. They are not imitators, these artists of London's only Victorian theatre; in their own right they have made for themselves and out of themselves a part of that bygone age. And surely they are in their rightful place beneath the arches, making themselves heard over the rumble of the coaches of "The London, Chatham and Dover Railway". As the Chairman and the more vociferous members of the audience nightly put it: "To hell with the London, Chatham and Dover Railway", and any of the "sleepers" who are not "awake" are surely wakened by these roaring choruses.

In arguing thus, there is no intention to decry the war years in that West End "billet". The success of the *Joys* there was real and complete in that place *and time*. But times are perpetually changing, and we with them. Because of the fine sentiments sincerely attaching to that earlier period in the development of the Players', people are sometimes slow to believe that which, when seen, confounds the idea that today's *Joys* will not stand up to yesterday's.

Don't you believe it. They will, and do.

Inheriting, as they did, the site of the building where Gatti's, one of London's most famous music-halls, once flourished, the Players' also inherited the last fading notes of those other artists whose friendly ghosts are not too disturbed by all the changes that have taken place. One *attended* at Gatti's – the interior hall with its architectural scheme was more like a Quaker's Meeting House than a hall of music and laughter. A gallery ran round the wall, and when it was packed with its audience, as it nearly always was, "it seemed that the Last Chairman had begun to beam from his pulpit upon the congregation and the choir" (*From Theatre to Music Hall*, by W. R. Titterton). When Gatti's flourished, all classes of people got drunk together, and the coster girl drank from the grocer's tankard with relish, and they sang gaily together, free of speech and of gesture, brothers and sisters in a night of enjoyment. Choruses were sung over and over again, and artists were sent off with the audience clapping themselves and shouting: "Well done, us!" There was a small band that accompanied the singers, "got up regardless", bashing at the drums, while the cornet players raised the roof, and again chorus after chorus going with a rip and a roar, and a rollicking time being had by all. The audience were as much performers as the artists at Gatti's, where, if they were not given what they wanted, they took it. The crowds went there to sing choruses, drink foaming ale from deep tankards, smoke until the vast place was blue with it, and squeeze their best girls – and be happy.

These are the pleasant shades of a far yesterday which had a long and, I feel sure, unasked-for rest before their home was taken over again by others who would inhabit the place of their friends, people they would recognise, songs they would remember, and maybe sing in their ghostly "voices".

Gatti's Hungerford Palace of
Varieties
after W. R. Sickert c 1888.

The Cave and the Garden was the first play produced by Leonard Sachs in the new premises. Of the production *The Times* critic wrote: "Once more there is Mr. Reginald Woolley's ingenious décor. The company keep the several facets simultaneously sparkling . . . the scene between Miss Sheila Burrell and Miss Julia Lang in the last act attains to beauty." "An evening of rare enchantment" (*Daily Telegraph*). "The play coaxes an old tale into new and glowing life" (J. C. Trewin in *Observer*). "Its action is no stronger than a flower; but, like a flower, it is ingeniously contrived" (*Sunday Times*). "Leonard Sachs gave the production a touch of magic" (*The Stage*). But the play lost money, despite the obviously well-deserved experiment.

In the two years that followed under the management of Leonard Sachs, the policy of giving new plays and revues was tried. His last production – a revue, *Players, Please* – was put on at the end of 1947, in place of the usual Christmas pantomime, with Joan Sterndale Bennett, Vida Hope, John Hewer, Bill Rowbotham, Hattie Jacques, Eleanor Summerfield and Diana Maddox. "Times change, and some Christmas entertainments with them. The theatre under the arches of Hungerford Bridge . . . no longer puts a slightly derisive swirl upon the crinoline" (*The Times*). "It is just the thing to go with the auditorium beer-sipping, a heartily arty, uninhibited show!" (*Daily Mail*). Mr. Alan Dent agreed: "It is often genuinely witty, and still oftener genuinely pretty both in its tunes and in its settings." Finally: "Scene after scene in its present revue is put on with a compelling evocativeness . . . in fact, if you really believe that either lack of money or official regulations are an excuse for indifferent work on the musical stage – go to the Players' Theatre" (Harold Hobson, *Sunday Times*).

However, from the box-office it became evident that one of the reasons for the survival of the Players' was the continued revival of Victorian music-hall. Leonard, who for sometime had been devoting himself to radio and the production of plays, decided to resign his director-ship, and in doing so to hand the theatre over to his three most immediate colleagues, Don Gemmell, Reginald Woolley and Gervase Farjeon. This was done at a committee-meeting on November 1st, 1947, in, as the report says, "A spirit of complete friendliness".

For a time the normal programme of *Late Joys* continued, but in the autumn another revue, *What Goes On*, was tried by the new management. The book and lyrics were by Ronnie Hill and Peter Dion Titheradge. The cast included many of the regular *Joys* artists.

However, as the end of the year approached it was decided that this time a pantomime should fill the bill at Christmas – a revival of an earlier success at Albemarle Street, *The Sleeping Beauty in the Wood*. There were some important changes in the cast from the previous production, but the whole dish went down succulently. "This handsome specimen of the Victorian pantomime is the verbal equivalent of the circus. . . . Miss Hattie Jacques must surely be among the funniest fairies . . . the two other particular joys of the entertainment are Miss Sterndale Bennett's Bad Fairy, who has such a disappointing time at the Christmas Party, and Mr. Bill Shine's absurd Irish woodcutter" (*The Times*). "The result is all that intimate pantomime should be . . . the Players' are equal to all their material. Don Gemmell has produced very nicely" (*Daily Telegraph*). "Reginald Woolley has designed some attractive period back-cloths which capture the essence of the legend, and at the same time suggest vast space on this bandbox stage . . . music ingeniously chosen . . . Hattie Jacques must have a larger heart than any other pantomime fairy . . . certainly the best of the Christmas shows" (*Stage*).

A tiny, pathetic note from Mr. Alan Dent: "People are gradually becoming too ready-of-wit to make my life much longer endurable. Amid nocturnal gaddings-about, I telephoned the Players' Theatre to ask if they had 'anything on' there. 'Of course, we've always something on here,' came the nimble answer. 'Who do you think we are – the Windmill?' " (*News Chronicle*).

Mr. Dent followed that call with a visit late on a January evening, and found "a crowded house, an endearing Hattie Jacques, a mock-miserable and unspeakable Philip Godfrey . . . and we all joined in the heckling of that elegant Chairman, Bill Shine". He was kind enough to add that the Players' was a club well worth joining – "if enjoying yourself late at night does not seem to you altogether too continental, too un-English". People were joining too. By March 1949, the membership was increasing. The *Joys* were steady favourites with the audience, who almost lifted the roof off the vast, packed arch of the theatre, with the old choruses and of course many "new" ones. In the middle of June another new play was tried out, *From This Day Forward*, by Kenlis Taylour. Although it did not make money for the Players' or the author, the theatre was living up to one of its purposes, to encourage dramatists and actors who had still to establish themselves on the public stage.

"From This Day Forward" – A Farmhouse in the Auvergne district

The pantomime this year, Christmas 1949, was *Beauty and The Beast*. For many weeks before it went on, there were comings and goings from wardrobe to stage of those making the costumes; Reggie browsing in the office through enormous books of drawings and paintings, and making notes and fascinating half-sketches that resolve themselves in the completed costumes and scenery; Don at rehearsals showing nothing of his easy, bluff casualness, nor yet, be it added, of the temperamental temper so often associated with producers. Indeed, his patience and politeness, particularly to young, earnest performers, seems thoroughly in keeping with, well – Victorian manners!

Hattie Jacques (the Marrygolda of that year) taking everything in her stride, carrying her enormous hand-bag that could contain half the sets and does contain heaven knows what, mislaying her script, leaving a valuable camera on the settee in the foyer, always losing something, seldom ruffled (tough when she is!), learning her part sitting in the box-office, over staff dinners, downstairs, upstairs, in taxis and dashing off to recordings of B.B.C. programmes in between; eternally smoking. Joan Sterndale Bennett – she was Dressalinda in that year – almost solemn, but as quick to smile as a child; unobtrusive in approach, "J.S.B.", who has been with the Players' since very shortly after its beginning in 1937, has shown the strength of all her funny wickedness and malicious satire in number after number, as indeed she has portrayed that other side, the winsome that can never quite hide its delight in the results. Johnnie Heawood, with all the seeming affectations of the stage-struck amateur, who has deceived so many people with his piercing voice and mannerisms; an artist to his finger-tips, an exhaustive artist who can never stop learning or practising, keenly sensitive and provoking in imagination, with a heart as deep as the deepest well, who can keep a table or a room in an uproar, and whose playing of the Harlequin in the Harlequinade following *Beauty and The Beast* had nothing of the meretricious and everything that was a pathetic delight. So one could go on, for they are all of them at the Players' artists of one degree or another. Everyone occupied with everything big and small that had the slightest connection with the approaching Christmas pantomime was occupied intensely, with a concentration that threw its own spell over the theatre.

As usual, on the Monday before the opening of the pantomime on December 20th, the theatre and club was closed and the day given over to lighting and full-dress rehearsals. The following night, with every seat packed in the house, the curtain went back before the expectant audience on what one newspaper described as: "A simple, ingenious, affective and altogether delightful show" (*Daily Telegraph*). The "Entirely New Stage Machinery and Novel Effects by Mr. G. Farjeon" excited comment here and there in the heads and hearts of Fleet Street and beyond, and the reviews thoroughly approved Don Gemmell's magnificent production. As *The Times* put it: "To those who have watched the progress of the Players' Theatre from its cramped but enthusiastic beginnings in Covent Garden 14 years ago, it has been one of the developing joys to study the gradual victory of the Victorian spirit over the wits who originally set out to caricature it. This year's pantomime is played more nearly 'straight' than ever before, and to that extent more successfully. The company leads the audience in giving itself up wholeheartedly to laughing, not at, but with J. R. Planché in his outrageously crude puns and rough-and-ready mockery. Very curiously the effect is to allow simple sentiment over and over again to get under the guard of sophistication."

Mr. Stephen Williams was both surprised and pleased – "One begins to wish oneself back with the Victorians, instead of purring in a smug intellectual superiority" (*Evening News*).

The *Manchester Guardian* chiding the theatre for "ideas that have sometimes been more praiseworthy than their performance" and "a style of production . . . occasionally condescending", fell under the spell of Beauty's beauty and Beast's romance, and assured Mr. Gemmell that his production was "charming".

The members, with their hundreds of guests, took the whole show to their hearts night after night for weeks. With a little more seriousness, as becomes them, the children enjoyed their special matinées, and sensibly pointed out the faults to each other, with every imaginable sort of improvement. In a previous pantomime one very solemn seven-year-old gave a most helpful piece of advice to the Clown in the Harlequinade (Mr. Archie Harradine): "If", she assured him gravely, "if you were to put bits of cardboard in your mouth and waggle them, and had strings with beads on hanging from your ears, I think you'd look terribly pretty!"

A particular event in the list of the Players' was the visit of the Princess Margaret. It was the evening of Queen Victoria's birthday that Her Highness chose, and so unobtrusive was her visit that many people did not know that she was there. The Princess "joined gaily in the songs, laughed heartily at the Chairman and watched the cake in honour of Queen Victoria being cut" (*Evening Standard* and *Evening News*). Don Gemmell confesses that the evening held its terrors for him as Chairman!

Steadily through the year the Players' spread its wings, with two broadcasts, one from the theatre and one from the studios. Television followed, and was judged to be "quite good entertainment, although we saw too little of the artists and too much of the audience" (*Evening News*). Even the *Nassau Guardian*, itself established in the reign of Queen Victoria, commented that "Her very Late Majesty, not easily amused, headed an era that now provides one of London's loudest laughs". A notice that might have been put a little more clearly, though most kindly in intent, appeared at this time in the *West Indian News* to the effect that "The little place of entertainment tucked away under Railway Arches burlesques Victorian music-hall. The audience consists mainly of people who come often. They know the words backwards, which is very necessary". Necessary or not, they certainly came often, the valued compliment to the Players' as a club, and the old familiar faces one sees three and four times in the same week are the regulars who teach the younger and newer members the long-established retorts to the Chairman's bantering. Some critics and Covent Garden members have complained that the elegance and the wit of earlier days has gone. This may be so, but the present Players' approaches nearer to the old type of music-hall.

Ali Baba and the Thirty-nine Thieves was the pantomime for 1950. This pantomime was discovered by Reginald Woolley in the British Museum, and copied out in long-hand.

The Times informed new members of the Players' that, "if they had any real title to be elected, they would appreciate the rollicking, knock-about fun, the brisk burlesque of grand opera, the cascades of excruciating rhymes fetched from the end of the earth and the dictionary. If the version presented is not absolutely authentic mid-Victoria, it would be an acute critic who could be sure where the classical text breaks off and the modern interpolations are

slipped in. Pace of production is of course the secret of the infectious appeal, and for that the credit belongs to Mr. Don Gemmell". Here the writer pays a most direct, deserved and charming tribute to "our own" J. S. B.: "Habituées will eagerly and rightly give the first honours to Miss Joan Sterndale Bennett. She has carried the chief burden of the *Joys* for so many years of peace and war; and now the latest joy is to acclaim her as she doubles the parts of principal boy and part author – a dashing blade and an ingenious poet". Hattie Jacques was, of course, the other half of the adaptation of H. J. Byron's *Ali Baba*. Mr. Youngman Carter of the *Tatler and Bystander* was satirically sarcastic when, after saying of the production that it was "the best thing of the season, rich in doggerel verse and outrageous puns", went on, "furthermore, should you be so disposed, you may carry drinks from the bar during the performance and consume them from the table by your chair. Whether the Lord Chamberlain does right to tolerate such public licence (even in a Theatre Club) is questionable. At the same time I feel bound to put on record that though some of the audience sang raucously, there was no sign of debauch, and the whole company gave the appearance of enjoying itself profoundly. Perhaps some good way of suppressing this sort of organised levity, which is out of character to foreign eyes, will be found before the opening of the Festival of Britain. In the meantime, here is the true spirit of pantomime".

The Festival of Britain set the pace, as it were, for all the activities of 1951. The idea was

DAPHNE ANDERSON

[Gregory

[Feldman

NUNA DAVEY
ARCHIE
HARRADINE

[Keystone

LYN EVANS

[Gregory

[Barry Hicks

EDRIC CONNOR

[Andrey Andersson

CHARLOTTE BIDMEAD

[Briggs

BERNARD MILES

[Anthony Stuart

JOHN HEWER and
DENIS MARTIN

[Feldman

BILL SHINE

[Keystone

ERIK CHITTY

[Picture Post

HATTIE JACQUES and
JOHN HEAWOOD

[Archer Photographic Co.

JEAN ANDERSON

PHILIP GODFREY

[Feldman

[Picture Post

80

conceived of presenting a scena which would depict Her Majesty Queen Victoria opening the Great Exhibition of 1851. Diana Morgan wrote the script and Mai Zetterling, at that time playing at the Duke of York's theatre in *Point of Departure*, was asked to take the part of the young Queen. It was one of the most delightfully dressed and decorated scenas presented at the theatre. Denis Wood took the part of the Prince Consort. Erik Chitty's Archbishop, Geoffrey Dunn's Duke of Wellington and Geoffrey Hibbert's mysterious Chinaman, with a large company of the *Joys*, made of it an impressive sight.

Timing was the most important part of that evening, timing to the minute, for the idea was to have the re-enactment take place as the chimes of Big Ben pealed out midnight, so that when the whole country welcomed the beginning of the Great Festival of Britain, 1951, the Players' Theatre would welcome the opening of the Great Exhibition of 1851. Arrangements were minutely detailed, and Miss Zetterling was brought from her theatre immediately the curtain came down. The *Joys* were still on, and the packed auditorium, overflowing from the seats to the dozens standing around the walls, grew quiet after the end of the programme, waiting, chatting with each other, glancing again and again at the drawn curtains as the hour of midnight approached.

Don Gemmell was conscious that although the programme of the opening of the 1851 Exhibition was a short one, this was an "occasion" at the Players', and as so often happens when his seriousness gets across the house, the sense of excitement caught the 300 who jammed the seats and bar, gangways and even the steps at each side of the stage, as he came on from the wings and made the announcement briefly and very simply.

This was the shortest of Don Gemmell's productions – it lasted barely fifteen minutes – it was certainly the most impressively exciting; and it is a pity that the Press, engaged elsewhere on that Festival Eve, did not see this solemn little celebration. However, a film record had been made of the scene by Gaumont British and is now in their archives.

It is pleasant to recall another production introducing Ruby Miller to the Players' audience, with its charming memories of the Gaiety Theatre in George Edwardes' time.

The scene reconstructed Ruby Miller's flat at the end of her performance of *Going Up* in 1918. Hattie Jacques, John Hewer, Johnnie Heawood, Charlotte Bidmead, Geoffrey Hibbert, Norman Warwick and Jean Ireland, all "her friends", hide as she comes in, followed by her valet carrying her skip of memories. The scene is quiet for a moment, then the lights are switched on and she finds herself surrounded by them. They implore her to reawaken her memories of those early days. Here again, the production was faultless, recapturing, with Ruby Miller's astonishing youthfulness the crest of the period. "John Hewer's rendering of the emotional ballad 'He was Right!' is one of the richest gems of the occasion" (*Tatler*). "Miss Charlotte Bidmead singing 'Take Me for a Game of Golf, Take Me for a Walk', evokes the graceful vision that was Phyllis Dare. The songs are a delightful reminder that Shaftesbury Avenue once held its own with Broadway. An entrancing evening" (*New Statesman*). "Miss Hattie Jacques, Mr Norman Warwick, Miss Charlotte Bidmead, Mr. Geoffrey Hibbert, and other clever members of the company sing most of the other songs from these Edwardian successes" (*The Times*). "The memories of the tunes of earlier days – from 'Our

Miss Gibbs', 'Theodora', 'The Orchid', and so on, are evoked by the discovery of an old wardrobe basket. The device is transparent, the sentiment lush, but the songs are worth reviving, and the players catch the antique style neatly enough" (*Manchester Guardian*). "Few artists can have had such a reception. Not only was the applause deafening, but the house rose at the end to do homage to her" (*Scotsman*). "A genial obeisance to 'modernity' by the Players' Theatre into the Edwardian, or perhaps the George Edwardesian, era has stirred up as fine a froth of reminiscence as London has enjoyed for a long time" (*Glasgow Herald*). And so on and so on. Not mentioned in the titles above are songs from *The Orchid* ("Come Along to the Zoo"), from *Theodora & Co.* ("Every Little Girl can teach Me Something New"), from *Our Miss Gibbs* ("Moonstruck" and "The Dudes Chorus"). What a night that was! Recollection followed recollection, and the famous story of the Indian prince who drank champagne from Ruby Miller's slipper has been told over and over again. Oh, the hansoms and the mashers that one could picture waiting at the stage-door as the whole cast, with Ruby in the middle, danced the final chorus from *Going Up*. It brought the house down and the show ended with rapturous applause. In the middle of the run, Ruby celebrated her sixty-second birthday. This was probably the most exhausting production the cast of the *Joys* had ever taken part in – Ruby Miller seemed to thrive on it!

The year 1951 came to an end with another Planché pantomime, and a New Year's Eve Party in which it seemed that every one of the three thousand odd members was present, for the theatre was packed almost to suffocation. *Riquet With the Tuft*, based on a "Grand Comical, Allegorical, Magical, Musical Burlesque Burletta", by J. R. Planché, was adapted by Hattie Jacques and Joan Sterndale Bennett,

As usual, Betty Lawrence and Stan Edwards took alternate weeks at the grand pianoforte, faithfuls of the *Joys* (in Betty's case) since Albemarle Street days and for the past four years in Stan's.

It had a formidable cast, with Erik Chitty as King Albert, Jean Anderson as Amy his Queen; Daphne Anderson as the Princess Allfair; Mdlle Violetta as Myrtilla, a "familiar" at the Court; Charles Lloyd Pack as Lord Chamberlain (even more familiar); Prince Riquet with the Tuft, Stephen Blake; Prince Finikin, John Hewer (both suitors for the hand of Princess Allfair). These comprised the "Mortals" in the pantomime. The "Immortals" were Hattie Jacques as Fairy Queen, Joan Sterndale Bennett as Fay Daze (always in one); Johnnie Heawood as Pixie Hood (a rummy spirit, well watered).

"The Players' Victorian pantomime this year is a two hours' spell of enchantment. Filled as it is with rhyming couplets, whispered asides, 'fashionable exit lines', amusingly strained plays upon words, the fragrant sentiment of melodious songs, the Gothic summer-houses and fairy pavilions – these are but some of the ingredients that contribute to the pleasure of the evening. Don Gemmell's polished production and Reginald Woolley's lusciously romantic settings suggest that these two artists have fallen completely under the spell of this Victorian fantasy, which they have staged in exquisite taste for our delight" (*The Stage*). "Daphne Anderson this year is, most happily, a Princess Charming; Joan Sterndale Bennett, a slightly dazed fairy, hovers and dithers to our delight – if not to the delight of her almost Gilbertian Fairy Queen (Hattie Jacques)" (*The Observer*). "It is delightfully sung, acted and staged and . . . I suspect that Hattie Jacques and her co-author introduced most of the wit into this jolly diversion" (*New Statesman*).

The sudden, tragic death of His Majesty the King, with all its saddening repercussions, naturally had its effect on the Players', and in a very real sense. It is the nightly custom at the beginning of a performance of *Late Joys* for the audience, at the invitation of the Chairman, to stand and drink a toast to Queen Victoria. This is the prelude to the commencement of the programme. For the first time since Don Gemmell had brought in this little custom, some eighteen months before, the toast was immediately cancelled, and was not pledged again until the night following the funeral of His Majesty. On that night, and ever since, a special and very real significance attaches itself to his call for a toast to "The Queen", as glasses and tankards are raised and the members echo "The Queen – God Bless Her", drinking the health of a memory and of a great lady on the throne of England today.

We understand that we are not Victorians, yet within a few minutes of the interchange of repartee between Chairman and ourselves we find ourselves back in that era.

You cannot stay outside this show, you cannot sit back and wait to be served with your entertainment, the pathos, the sentiment and the fun. Here, at the Players', we are astonished at the vast strides made in railway communications; they almost encircle London and its suburbs; Roake and Varty's shop at the top of Villiers Street—you passed it on your way here—has only just got its demolition orders, so that the approaches can be made to the big new station called Charing Cross.

Whisky, as you know, is going up, and now costs three-and-six the bottle, and as for coal at fifteen shillings the ton, what is the Government doing about the constant rise in prices? And Income Tax at fivepence in the pound! But no matter, we will forget the high cost of things and listen to "Your own EVER-ADORABLE . . . Nuna . . . DAVEY" singing:

"*Now isn't it a pity such a pretty girl as I*
Should be cooped up in a nunnery to pine away and die.
I'm sure I cannot tell now what the mischief I have done,
But my mother often tells me I must be a nun."

With its flirtingly defiant chorus of

"*But I* won't *be a nun, no, I* won't *be a nun;*
I am *so fond of pleasure that I can-not be a nun!*"

Here in the atmosphere of mutton-chop whiskers, heavy moustaches, hot pies, hot dogs and glasses of beer, her demure stubbornness is exactly right, and when the hoarse, ripe, lusty voice of Chairman Don Gemmell calls for our "customary warmth of welcome" for that darling of the *Joys*, Hattie Jacques, who is going to perform something about a cock linnet, there is a roar of applause as she comes on from the wings – there's a don't-give-a-darn air about her that is sheer delight and a brawling boisterousness that sends the choruses ringing to the roof.

During the "short interval for refreshments", the bars in the auditorium and supper-room are crowded and conversation all over the theatre is loud. There's a plentiful passing of pints of beer from row to row, with plates of hot-dogs, sandwiches and coffee to fill the tables in readiness for the second part of the entertainment, which begins with an artist whose activities as a Central European spy has filled volumes – Vida Hope, with her "Diary of Madam X", told in phrases redolent of Kensington Gore that regrettably slip into the tones of the very worst part of Camden Town. Her "revelations" are vastly enjoyable, her dignity only occasionally shaky. Philip Godfrey with his guitar and his song of the Roving Tinker sets our feet tapping, and of course he has to come back and give us another. Fred Stone strides briskly on to the stage, waiting for, demanding and getting enough applause for ten artists before he starts to enchant us with "The Bosom Friend of Albert Prince of Wales", and going off only

after he has applauded himself with shouts of delight! They are all here, the good old-timers, and one after another they come from the wings, delights of the reign of Queen Victoria, our delights. We know them, we like them, we love them, and always they move us, to excitement, to laughter, to sentiment, and sometimes very near to tears.

Harold Scott, who had produced the first *Late Joys* programme for Peter Ridgeway, and who had had his own "Cave of Harmony" (with Elsa Lanchester) in the 1920's and had also written a book on the Supper Rooms and Music Halls, came once again to the Players' with his own adaptation of *The Castle Spectre*, by M. G. "Monk" Lewis, a late eighteenth-century Gothic melodrama.

The Castle Spectre was first performed at the Theatre Royal, Drury Lane, in 1797, where it played for sixty successive nights. Eighty years later it was revived. Now it was to be revived again. The cast, led by Edmund Willard, consisted of Milton Rosmer, Brian Oulton, Mary Laura Wood, Don Gemmell, May Hallatt and Philip Godfrey, with Prudence Rennick as the Spectre itself.

"The Castle Spectre"
— A Subterraneous Place —

THE CASTLE SPECTRE;
A DRAMATIC ROMANCE IN FIVE ACTS.—BY M. G. LEWIS.

Act IV.—Scene 2.

CHARACTERS.

OSMOND	MOTLEY	MULEY	HAROLD
REGINALD	KENRIC	ALARIC	ANGELA
PERCY	SAIB	ALLAN	ALICE
FATHER PHILIP	HASSAN	EDRIC	EVELINA

ACT I.—SCENE I. *A Grove.*
Enter FATHER PHILIP *and* MOTLEY *through a gate.*

F. Phil. Never tell me. I repeat it, you are a fellow of a very scandalous course of life. But what principally offends me is, that you pervert the minds of the maids, and keep kissing and smuggling all the pretty girls you meet. Oh! fie! fie!

Mot. I kiss and smuggle them? St. Francis forbid! Lord love you, Father, 'tis they who kiss and smuggle me. I protest I do what I can to preserve my modesty; and I wish that Archbishop Dunstan had heard the lecture upon chastity which I read last night to the dairy-maid in the dark; he'd have been quite edified. But yet what does talking signify? The eloquence of my lips is counteracted by the lustre of my eyes; and really, the little devils are so tender, and so troublesome, that I'm half angry with nature for having made me so very bewitching.

F. Phil. Nonsense! nonsense!

Mot. Put yourself in my place. Suppose that a sweet; smiling rogue, just sixteen, with rosy cheeks, sparkling eyes, pouting lips, &c.—

F. Phil. Oh! fie! fie! fie! To hear such licentious discourse brings the tears into my eyes!

Mot. I believe you, Father; for I see the water is running over at your mouth; which puts me in mind, my good Father, that there are some little points which might be altered in you still better than in myself: such as intemperance, gluttony—

F. Phil. Gluttony! Oh! abominable falsehood!

Mot. Plain matter of fact! Why, will any man pretend to say that you came honestly by that enormous belly, that tremendous tomb of fish,

flesh, and fowl? And, for incontinence, you must allow yourself, that you are unequalled.

F. Phil. I!—I!—

Mot. You; you. May I ask what was your business in the beech-grove, the other evening, when I caught you with buxom Margery, the miller's pretty wife? Was it quite necessary to lay your heads together so close?

F. Phil. Perfectly necessary: I was whispering in her ear wholesome advice, and she took it as kindly as I gave it.

Mot. So you was, faith! Father; you gave it with your lips, and she took it with her's. Well done, Father Philip!

F. Phil. Son, son, you give your tongue too great a license.

Mot. Nay, Father, be not angry: fools, you know, are privileged persons.

F. Phil. I know they are very useless ones; and, in short, master Motley, to be plain with you, of all fools I think you the worst; and for fools of all kinds I've an insuperable aversion.

Mot. Really! Then you have one good quality at least, and I cannot but admire such a total want of self-love! (*Bell rings.*) But, hark! there goes the dinner-bell. Away to table, Father. Depend upon't, the servants will rather eat *part* of their dinner unblessed, than stay 'till your stomach comes, like Jonas's whale, and swallows up the *whole.*

F. Phil. Well, well, fool; I am going; but first let me explain to you that my bulk proceeds from no indulgence of voracious appetite. No, son, no. Little sustenance do I take; but St. Cuthbert's blessing is upon me, and that little prospers with

The notices of this collector's piece give it the serious consideration it deserved. "The revival, staged sincerely, was received light-heartedly, as if it were 'old fashioned' melodrama. Its deserts were somewhat higher, though the 'goings-on' did make large demands on the talents of the players and the imagination of the audience" (*Daily Telegraph*). "Rescued from some dusty theatrical limbo and played as near seriously as actors could manage. . . . Perilously fustian stuff . . . altogether a diverting evening, whose principal honours were shared by Edmund Willard and Reginald Woolley, whose sets were a triumph of ingenuity and truly Gothic melancholy" (*Evening News*). "How do you set about burlesquing a burlesque?" asked Mr. Harold Conway of the *Evening Standard*, and went on to say: " 'Monk' Lewis this time was stooping rather than spooking, and the joke fell a trifle uncertainly. The author had enjoyed the last laugh – 150 years ago".

It remains to be seen what will happen in the future. One thing is quite certain, experiments and variations will come and go every once in a while – but the *Joys* will go on for ever. This is the yard-stick of the success of the Players'; the bond between artists and members is a secure and a friendly one, by virtue of the *Joys* being part of the audience and the audience being part of the programme.

This is the story of how the Players' Theatre came into being; how it grew branches from a trunk only sixteen years old. Young, really, but the roots are steeped in Time, in a hundred years of time, far back into that other age, those days of yet another great Queen, under whose reign there flourished the Supper Room of "Evans's – Late Joys".

[Photo Arts
URSULA

[Gregory

[Photo Arts
EDNA HEWER

Signing in
[Picture Post

[Polyfoto
GERVASE FARJEON

[Photo Arts
REGINALD WOOLLEY

[Photo Arts
DON GEMMELL

[Picture Post
ANDY

[Picture Post
TED

[Picture Post
"Dear Old Pals"

SCENAS

[Andrey Andersson
Daddy's on the Engine

RUBY MILLER in Gaiety Memories

The Streets of London

Middle West Saloon Bar

[Photos: Feldman

List of Plays, etc.

Date	Title	Author, Producer	Cast included:
1936			
18 October	*In a Balcony*	Robert Browning Leonard Sachs	Kate Cutler, Leonard Sachs, Cicely Paget-Bowman
	Love Scene	Patricia Hayes	Rosalind Atkinson, P. Hayes, Robert Eddison, June Wenner, Leonard Sachs
	A Brown Woman	James B. Cabell Leonard Sachs	Peter Ridgeway, Holland Bennett
	Excalibur	Clare Hope	
1937			
27 December (1936) and	*Variety*		Margaret Leona, Patricia Hayes, Leonard Sachs and Gwynne Whitby
3 January	*I made you Possible*	Ivor Brown	Rosalind Atkinson
1 January	*Roel Puppets*		
8 January	*Renatah Kuh : Dance Recital*		
17 January	*Laura, the Do-as-you-like Girl*	Anne Ridgeway	Brian Colman, June Wenner, Rosalind Atkinson, Anne Ridgeway, Louise Hampton, Patricia Hayes
	Love Scene	Patricia Hayes	Peter Ridgeway, Senior and Junior
	The House with the Column	Pirandello Peter Ridgeway	Robert Eddison, Leonard Sachs, Julian Somers
7 February	*Renatah Kuh: Dance Recital*		
12 February	*South African Night*	Leonard Sachs	Irving Kaye, Nan Munro, Miriam Stein
23 February	Lydian Trio		
2 March	*Variety*		Margaret Leona, Maisie Seneshall and Valentine Rooke
15 March	Croydon Theatre Guild		
9 April	*Ruby Morn*	Charles Landstone Peter Ridgeway	Winifred Evans, Ena Moon, Malcolm Morley, Laurence Hanray, Campbell Logan, Dan Tobin
18 April	*Human Straws*	Peter Rogers	
27 April	*Friends, Romans . . .* (revue)	L. Julian Jones and Maurice Samuel Peter Ridgeway	
21 May	*To the Poets of Australia*	H. F. Rubinstein	Janet Barrow
	Sicilian Limes	Pirandello Ida Teather	Ambrosine Philpotts
	Out Goes She	Philip Johnson	Leonard Sachs, Frank Napier, Alex. Sarner
25 May	*Waiting for Lefty*	Unity Theatre production	
3 June	Ebor Marionettes		
18 June	*The Antirrhinum is a Lovely Thing*	Ralph Baker	Viola Tree, Hazel Terry, Wilson Barrett
22 September	*Down on the Farm*	Cecil Tailby Peter Ridgeway	Coral Fairweather, Janet Barrow, Frank Napier, Ben Wright
4 October	*Distant Fields*	S. K. Lauren Alec Clunes	Margaret Dunn, Helen Vayne, Mary Graham, John Ridley, Alan Aldridge, Oliver Gordon
8 October	*Panache* (variety)		Elinor Shân and Archie Harradine
23 October	*Lady Sarah's Bailiff*	Irene Garnett Peter Ridgeway	Janet Barrow, Patricia Hayes, May Hallatt, Kate Parker, Michael Osler, Frank Napier
27 October	*God's Jailer*	Geoffrey Thomas Leonard Sachs	Ernest Milton, Frank Napier, Eric Christmas, Campbell Logan, Philip Holles, Helen Vayne, Geoffrey Toone
	Tomorrow at Midnight	Martin Wilder Alec Clunes	
	and *Variety*		Maisie Seneshall, Pamela Glynne, Hazel Terry, Mira Devi, Elinor Shân, Eric Christmas, Peter Ridgeway, Leonard Sachs and Archie Harradine
11 November	*Panache*		
17 November	*Little Earthquake*	Beatrice Mayor Peter Ridgeway	Winifred Evans, Patricia Hayes, Coral Fairweather, Nan Munro, Robert Gilbert, Rule Pyott, Leonard Sachs, Philip Thornley, Norman Caro
24 November	*Character Sketches*		Elspeth Douglas-Reid
25 November	*Spanish Dancer*		Marjorie Dey
	Mezzo-soprano		Ivy Dey

Date	Title	Author, Producer	Cast included:
1937 4 December	*Little Earthquake*	Beatrice Mayor Peter Ridgeway	Winifred Evans, Patricia Hayes, Coral Fairweather, Nan Munro, Robert Gilbert, Rule Pyott, Leonard Sachs, Philip Thornley
6 December	EVANS'S LATE JOYS produced by Harold Scott		
29 December	*Ridgeway's Late Joys*		Lea Seidl, Gabrielle Brune, Megs Jenkins, Patricia Hayes, Virginia Winter, Eve Lynd, Peter Ridgeway, Eric Christmas, Richard Haydn, Tony Spurgin, John Rudling, Ben Wright, Philip Thornley
1938 18 January	*The Boots at the Swan*	Charles Selby Willson Disher	Valentine Rooke, Leonard Sachs, Eileen Way, Campbell Logan, Patricia Hayes
22 February	*Heaven and Charing Cross*	Aubrey Danvers-Walker Peter Ridgeway	Olive Walter, Jean Shepheard
7 March	(Transferred to Garrick Theatre)		Helen Goss, Megs Jenkins, Marjorie Rhodes, Christine Hartley, Brian Hayes, Maurice Denham, Ben Wright, Philip Thornley
25 March	Players' Mixture : *William's Other Anne* *Exile* and *Variety*	Ivor Brown Leonard Sachs	Hazel Terry, Leonard Sachs, David King-Wood, James Parrish, Patricia Hayes, Christine Silver, Kitty de Legh, Deirdre Doyle, Marcella Salzer, Elinor Shán, Biddy Walker, Archie Harradine
28 April	*Charles and Mary*	Joan Temple Peter Ridgeway	Joan Temple and Peter Ridgeway, Janet Barrow, Winifred Evans, Patricia Hayes, Marjorie Rhodes, Christine Hartley, Ruth Reeves, Maurice Denham, John Ruddock, Frith Banbury, Stringer Davis, Hugh Burden, Sidney Young
24 May	*Club Sandwich* (variety)	John Hotchkiss Nicholson Soulsby Leonard Sachs	Frank Drew, Phillida Sewell, Eric Christmas, John Glyn-Jones, Edgar K. Bruce, Irving Kaye, Quit Holmgren
18 June	*Panache*		
11 July	*Lease for Disposal*	Campbell Logan Leonard Sachs	Josephine Dent, Molly Rankin, Emma Trechman, Stringer Davis, John Robinson, Alex. Sarner
26 October	*What next, Baby?*	A. G. Macdonell Leonard Sachs	Megs Jenkins, Ambrosine Philpotts, Emma Trechman, Molly Hamley-Clifford, Cyril Chamberlain, Bernard Miles, John Salew, Tony Quinn, Oliver Gordon, Arnold Riches, Fred Royal, Pat Susands
1939 1 February	*The Shoemaker's Last*	Geoffrey Thomas Leonard Sachs	Hazel Terry, Nuna Davey, Joan Sterndale Bennett, Helen Goss, Amy Dalby, Cyril Chamberlain, John Garside, John Salew, Michael Ashwin, Oliver Gordon
February	Columbia Album of 'Late Joys' Records issued.		
27 March	*Young Today*	Peter Powell Leonard Sachs	Renée Asherson, Marjorie Mars, Joan Sterndale Bennett, Caroline Bayley, Viola Johnstone, Margaret Leona, David Burney, Brian Hayes, Gordon Macleod, Martin Lewis, Geoffrey Waring, Katie Johnson
7 June	*Luck of the Devil*	Lynton Hudson from Fr. of Jean Letraz, music by Michael Sayer Leonard Sachs	José Huntley-Wright, Megs Jenkins, Molly Hartley-Milburn, Robert Eddison, David Keir, Don Gemmell, John Garside, William Hutcheson
18 December	*Whittington Jnr. and His Cat*	H. J. Byron and Robert Reece Adapted by Archie Harradine Leonard Sachs	Peter Ustinov, Archie Harradine, Arthur Burne, Lyn Evans, Nuna Davey, John Moody, Rosalind Atkinson, Barbara Mullen, Joan Sterndale Bennett, Don Gemmell
3 September	WAR DECLARED. Entertainments closed down.		
25 September	LATE JOYS re-open at the Arts Theatre.		
November	Return to King Street, Covent Garden.		
1940 September	Play for a week at Francis Iles' house, Hamilton Terrace, W		
October	Transfer to 13 Albemarle Street, W.		

Date	Title	Author, Producer	Cast included:
1941 22 December	*Whittington Jnr. and His Cat*	H. J. Byron and Robert Reece Adapted by Archie Harradine Leonard Sachs	Don Gemmell, Archie Harradine, Joan Gates, Arthur Burne, Audrey Teesdale, Nuna Davey, Jean Anderson, Joanna Horder, Joan Sterndale Bennett
1942 28 December	*St. George and the Dragon*	Adapted by Archie Harradine Don Gemmell	Joanna Horder, John Mott, Jean Anderson, Frank Baker, Harry Locke, Don Gemmell, Joan Sterndale Bennett, Charlotte Bidmead, Archie Harradine
1943 22 December	*Cinderella*	H. J. Byron Adapted by Archie Harradine Don Gemmell	Heather Boys, Charlotte Bidmead, Harry Locke, Archie Harradine, Jean Anderson, Paulette Preney, Joan Sterndale Bennett
1944 29 May	*In a Balcony*	Robert Browning Leonard Sachs	Leonard Sachs, Julia Lang, Jean Anderson
20 December	*The Sleeping Beauty in the Wood*	J. R. Planché Adapted by Archie Harradine Don Gemmell	Joan Sterndale Bennett, Archie Harradine, Don Gemmell, Jean Anderson, Jane Connard, Thérèse Langfield, Daphne Anderson, Hattie Jacques, Charlotte Bidmead, Diana Maddox, Bill Shine, Joanna Horder
1946 14 January	LATE JOYS re-open at Villiers Street, W.C.2		
24 March	Chamber Music		Blech Quartet, Frederick Thurston
24 April	*The Cave and the Garden*	Ormerod Greenwood Leonard Sachs	Sheila Burrell, Peter Burton, Raymond Westwell, Charlotte Bidmead, Daphne Anderson, Hattie Jacques, Pat Gilder, Julia Lang, John Longden, Don Gemmell, David Keir, Bill Shine, Frederick Bennett, John Franklyn, Joan Sterndale Bennett
30 June	Schubert Recital		Mary and Geraldine Peppin, Victor Carne, Hyman Sachs
25 September	*The Amiable Mrs. Luke*	Geoffrey Thomas Leonard Sachs	Peggy Attfield, Jane Connard, Bill Shine, Joan Sterndale Bennett, Norman Claridge, Phillada Sewell, Cicely Paget-Bowman, Owen Holder, Bill Rowbotham, Hattie Jacques, Merle Tottenham
23 December	*Cinderella*	H. J. Byron Adapted by Archie Harradine Don Gemmell	Elma Soiron, Joan Sterndale Bennett, Bill Shine, Owen Holder, May Hallatt, Joyce Cummings, Phillada Sewell, Thérèse Langfield, Marguerite Stewart
1947 12 January	Reading—*In a Balcony*	Robert Browning	Rosalind Atkinson, Julia Lang, Leonard Sachs
27 February– 4, 7, 11 March	Four Recitals		Edric Connor
11 June	*Calcutta in the Morning*	Geoffrey Thomas Leonard Sachs	John Longden, Joyce Cummings, Josephine Fraser, Winefrede Nelson, Neville Mapp, John Hewer, Beatrice Rowe, Brian Roper, Phillip Holles, Don Gemmell
9 December	*Players, Please* (revue)	Various Leonard Sachs	Ronnie Hill, Hattie Jacques, Bill Rowbotham, Joan Sterndale Bennett, Pamela Chrimes, Eleanor Summerfield, John Hewer, John Scarff, Vida Hope, Diana Maddox
31 December	Puppets	Hogarth Puppets	
1948 16 November	*What Goes On* (revue)	Ronnie Hill and Peter Dion Titheradge Ronnie Hill	Derek Hain, Michael Westmore, Joanna Horder, Eleanor Summerfield, Joan Sterndale Bennett, Iris Ballard, Ian Carmichael, Janet Bothwell, Cyril Wells, Peter Hawkins
21 December	*The Sleeping Beauty in the Wood*	J. R. Planché Adapted by Archie Harradine Don Gemmell	Joan Sterndale Bennett, Charlotte Bidmead, Clive Dunn, Don Gemmell, Jean Anderson, Hattie Jacques, Ursula Medley, Patricia Hartley, Bill Shine, William McAlpine, Violetta

Date	Title	Author, Producer	Cast included:
1949 20 June	*From This Day Forward*	Kenlis Taylour Harold Young	Brian Oulton, Douglas Jefferies, Peggy Thorpe-Bates, Victoria Grayson, Meadows White, Eileen Beldon, Bridgid Hodgson, Reginald Jarman, John Hewer, Anthony Bacon, Roger Williams, Daphne Hanson
20 December	*Beauty and the Beast*	J. R. Planché Adapted by Archie Harradine Don Gemmell	Daphne Anderson, Gavin Gordon, Erik Chitty, Bill Shine, John Heawood, Joan Sterndale Bennett, Hattie Jacques, Rose Hill, Charlotte Bidmead, Lisa Lee
1950 19 December	*Ali Baba or The Thirty-Nine Thieves*	H. J. Byron Adapted by Hattie Jacques and Joan Sterndale Bennett Don Gemmell	Erik Chitty, John Hewer, Don Gemmell, Joan Sterndale Bennett, Dennis Wood, John Heawood, Tony Sympson, Hattie Jacques, Daphne Anderson, Joy Holman
1951 1 May	*Apartments*	Brough Don Gemmell	Joan Sterndale Bennett, Erik Chitty, Hattie Jacques, John Heawood, Violetta, Dennis Wood, Don Gemmell
3 May	*The Crystal Palace—1851*	Diana Morgan Don Gemmell	Robert MacDermot, John Hewer, Archie Harradine, Clive Dunn, Mai Zetterling, Dennis Wood, Erik Chitty, Geoffrey Dunn, Geoffrey Hibbert, Hattie Jacques, Joan Sterndale Bennett, Lisa Lee, Joy Holman, Violetta, John Heawood, Stan Edwards, Norman Warwick
18 December	*Riquet with the Tuft*	J. R. Planché Adapted by Hattie Jacques and Joan Sterndale Bennett Don Gemmell	Erik Chitty, Jean Anderson, Daphne Anderson, Violetta, Charles Lloyd Pack, Stephen Blake, John Hewer, Edward Monson, Joan Gadsdon, Hattie Jacques, Joan Sterndale Bennett, John Heawood
1952 31 March	*The Castle Spectre*	M. G. Lewis Harold Scott	Edmund Willard, Milton Rosmer, Brian Oulton, Don Gemmell, Peter Bennett, Philip Godfrey, Michael Ingham, Harold Young, David Gideon Thomson, Mary Laura Wood, May Hallatt, Prudence Rennick

Appendix

VILLIERS STREET, THE DUKE'S THEATRE AND DAVID GARRICK

A Theory, with Repercussions

IT was whilst doing some casual research into the history of Villiers Street, the home of the present Players' Theatre, that I came across a reference to David Garrick that excited my curiosity, led me to delve a little further, and eventually to put forward a theory that interested *The Times* newspaper. Garrick, as we know, was a century earlier than our period here. At that time the Hungerford Market entrance at the bottom of Villiers Street fronted the river – the Charing Cross Underground Station has now replaced that remarkably beautiful building – and on top of the market were two taverns situated on each front corner. One of these, on the Villiers Street side, may well have been "The Swan", but admittedly one cannot be sure of this. However, a tavern was certainly pulled down on that corner in 1737, the year that David Garrick arrived in London, an actor at heart but a wine dealer in fact. He came from his home in Lichfield to open an office and storehouse in partnership with his brother, who remained in Lichfield. This was in Durham Yard, on the south side of the Strand near to Covent Garden. Because of the business that was carried on, but perhaps more because of his singularly pleasing personality, Garrick inevitably met many members of the theatrical profession. In the taverns and coffee-houses he soon became known as the friend and confidante of actors and actresses, and was often invited into the green rooms of the various theatres. Garrick had wanted to act ever since he was a child. He was "mad" about the theatre, and allowed the wine business at Durham Yard to deteriorate to such an extent that there were frequent quarrels between the brothers – Peter was six years older than David Garrick. Time and time again one comes across such references as the following: "Peter did not know that his associate in a respectable business was also the associate of actors and managers" . . . "Impelled by a secret passion he dared not divulge [he] had gone privately to Ipswich with the manager, Giffard, and under the name Lyddal had played" . . . "They were partners still, but David underwent sharp lectures from his grave senior on the impropriety of getting up theatrical squibs"; etc., etc., etc. (*Oliver Goldsmith's Life and Times*, by John Forster).

Garrick was not only frightened of his elder brother knowing of his love for acting, but

95

realised that – and this was strictly in keeping with the thought of the times – it would be "a shameful forfeiture of station which had lowered the son of a marching captain into a mean stage player" (Forster). Such tidings conveyed to his sedate and most respectable family in Lichfield would be ill news indeed.

It seemed to me, at an early stage of my enquiring, that there was some possibility of David Garrick having appeared on the London stage professionally long before it was officially known. His appearance is supposed to have been on October 19th, 1741. Wheatley's *London Past and Present* provided a further, though misleading clue. Here there is a reference to Garrick having in fact appeared at the "Duke's Theatre", in Villiers Street, towards the end of the year 1738, some three years before this accepted appearance of 1741.

This alone was interesting, and the fact that the street was that in which the Players' Theatre now delights the town added to it. Wheatley's reference was taken from a book he called *The Children of Thespis*, by one Anthony Pasquin. A long search followed through many editions of the work, without a single reference to Garrick being discovered. It seemed that yet another error – of the many one comes across in "authoritative" works – had been made, and that one's hope of an interesting and important "find" had been dashed. But not quite. Pasquin also wrote under the name Williams, and a quick search soon brought to light *The Pin Basket to the Children of Thespis*, with "Notes Historical, Critical and Biographical". The volume was published in 1797, eighteen years after the death of David Garrick. On page 208 the following is written: "About three years previously to Mr. Garrick's appearance at Goodmans-fields, he performed Chamont at a small theatre called the Duke's Theatre, in Villiers Street, York Buildings, which was situated within a few doors of the bottom of the street at the right-hand side. The play was got up by the scholars of Eton College, and was prompted by Colley Hill . . . the ladies who were present *at Mr. Garrick's professional début* [my italics] were so fascinated by his splendid powers, that they offered him their purses and trinkets from the boxes. The other characters were . . .", etc.

The evidence seemed now to point quite definitely to an appearance long before the one recorded and accepted for 1741. Pasquin's reference later on to the members of the cast, his comment on the ladies throwing their purses and trinkets on to the stage, seemed and seems too exact a statement to be ignored as merely faulty recollection, or as a deliberate, purposeful lie.

As to the existence of this Duke's Theatre in Villiers Street – it must have been opposite to the present Players' Theatre – there is plenty of evidence. I refer readers who are interested to W. Davenport Adams's *A Book about London*, published 1890: ". . . Villiers Street, Strand. Sir Richard Steele was a resident, in York Buildings, from 1715 to 1725, and built here his 'Censorium', a kind of hall intended, it would seem, for holding conversaziones, enlivened by songs, recitations and dramatic entertainments . . .". Steele left Villiers Street in 1725, following the death of his wife, the jealous Prue, and died in Wales four years later.

I can only presume that he left his "Censorium" there. What happened to it, or in it, in the thirteen years between Steele leaving the street and Garrick arriving in London, I do not know, despite intensive research. If it should seem to the reader that Davenport Adams was wrong, I can assure him that a reference can be found in *The Epistolatory Letters of Sir Richard*

Steele, at the British Museum, to Steele's anxiety over money to pay the workmen erecting the stage there.

Up to the time of this book going to press, I have not been able to trace any map or playbill of this theatre, at the Guildhall, the Royal Society of British Architects or the British Museum; yet that the theatre existed there is no doubt at all. The written references are clear. Now for the denial of this assumed appearance of Garrick in 1738. In Austin Brereton's *Literary History of the Adelphi and its Neighbourhood*, 1907, he writes: "On the sole authority of that wicked libeller and scurrillous writer, Anthony Pasquin, otherwise John Williams, 'one of the dirtiest and most disreputable fellows that ever disgraced the literary profession', it has been related that Garrick, three years before he appeared for the first time on the London stage, had acted in the Duke's Theatre, and that . . ." (here Brereton repeats the Pasquin observations about Garrick's reception). Brereton goes on: "This is not so, for Garrick did not play before the public in London until October 19th, 1741".

A denial, in all conscience; but not necessarily the last word. The facts are that Garrick wanted so much to be an actor that from the moment he arrived in London he began to neglect the business for which he had come there, to sell wine, neglected it to the extent of costing the concern over £400, while he became the friend of actors and used the green rooms as his clubs.

The Times took a hand in the matter on Saturday, April 19th, 1952, quoting the research I had done and the theory of this earlier appearance in 1738. Some three weeks later a letter was printed in the same newspaper, from Sir St. Vincent Troubridge, of the Garrick Club, emphatically denying my contention and quoting an unpublished wager of the year 1732, as follows:

"A wager in writing on the date of his first appearance on the professional stage. 'Mr Bedford Wagers two gallons of Claret with Mr Williams that Mr Garrick did not ply upon ye s^d Stage in ye Year 1732 or before . . . Paid. I acted upon Goodmans Fields theatre for ye first time in ye Year 1741. David Garrick. Witness, Somerset Draper ' ".

I find this wager interesting for two reasons. (1) It seems that even in 1732, there was sufficient conjecture about Garrick's first appearance for there to be a wager about it, and (2) Garrick's signing the wager as a true declaration *refers only to Goodmans-fields*, which appearance I am not foolish enough to deny. In any case, the evidence of Garrick's early life in London, his fears of his brother and for his family, who might hear that he wanted to be an actor, is far too strong to be casually dismissed. I think it very likely that among his actor friends around Covent Garden there were some who found the opportunity for the young Garrick to appear on the stage. Durham Yard, where he had his business, was quite near to Villiers Street. Finally, what made Giffard, his manager, offer him £300 per year for the 1741 appearance if he had not seen Garrick's professional abilities elsewhere? It was a large sum in those days, and Giffard was an astute business-man.

The ARTISTES include—

Jean Anderson
Daphne Anderson
Hedli Anderson
Alexander Archdale
Sydney Arnold
Rosalind Atkinson
Frank Baker
Frith Banbury
Charlotte Bidmead
Heather Boys
Ian Carmichael
Erik Chitty
Alec Clunes
Edric Connor
Joyce Cummings
Colleen Clifford
Nuna Davey

Geoffrey Dunn
Clive Dunn
Robert Eddison
Lyn Evans
Jonathan Field
Elsie French
Philip Godfrey
John Glyn Jones
May Hallatt
Archie Harradine
Elton Hayes
John Heawood
John Hewer
Geoffrey Hibbert
Owen Holder
Vida Hope

Joanna Horder
Hattie Jacques
Ernest Jay
Megs Jenkins
James Justice
John Justin
Lilly Kann
Irving Kaye
Julia Lang
Thérèse Langfield
Lisa Lee
Charles Leno
Harry Locke
Diana Maddox
Denis Martin
Bernard Miles

John Mott
Barbara Mullen
Robert Nichols
Ronan O'Casey
Peggy van Praagh
Bill Rowbotham.
Leonard Sachs
Bill Shine
Joan Sterndale Bennett
Fred Stone
Eleanor Summerfield
Tony Sympson
Peter Ustinov
Violetta
Josephine Wilson
Dennis Wood

Chairman :- Don Gemmell

At the pianoforte :- Betty Lawrence & Stan Edwards

Scenery designed and painted by REGINALD WOOLLEY
Stage Director : GERVASE FARJEON
Stage Manager : MARY BENNETT assisted by VERNON RUSSELL
Ballets arranged by JOHN HEAWOOD
Costumes by PLAYERS' THEATRE WARDROBE, L. & H. NATHAN, Ltd.
Nylon Stockings by KAYSER BONDOR
Stage Lighting by MAJOR EQUIPMENT Co., Ltd.
Master Carpenter : FREDERICK DRAPER
Secretary : ENID COLLETT
Box Office : EDNA HEWER

1952

Design by H. V. Stephenson